J. J. ROUSSEAU: AN AFTERLIFE OF WORDS

ELI FRIEDLANDER

Harvard University Press
Cambridge, Massachussetts
London, England
2004

Copyright © 2004 by the President and
Fellows of Harvard College
All rights reserved
Printed in the United States of America

Library of Congress Cataloging-in-Publication Data

Friedlander, Eli.
J.J. Rousseau : an afterlife of words / Eli Friedlander.
p. cm.
Includes bibliographical references and index.
ISBN 0-674-01514-2 (alk. paper)
1. Rousseau, Jean-Jacques, 1712–1778. Rêveries du promeneur solitaire. I. Title: J.J. Rousseau. II. Title.
PQ2040.R53F75   2004
848′.509—dc22   2004047387

To Omer, to Elam, to Michal

Acknowledgments

My initial impulse to write on Rousseau's *Reveries of the Solitary Walker* was occasioned by the preparation of a lecture for a conference entitled "Acknowledging Stanley Cavell." The topic of my lecture was in part decided by finding Rousseau's *Reveries* among a list of works Cavell refers to as spanning the dimensions of the outlook he calls Moral Perfectionism. That discovery only reinforced my growing sense that Cavell's writings provided an entry into Rousseau's text and gave me words to formulate my hitherto somewhat speechless attachment to the *Reveries*. Cavell's investment in my interest in Rousseau goes back to his care in advising my doctoral dissertation. In writing the present book, some years later, I realized the inner life of the many conversations we have had, feeling drawn to respond to him, to have my writing address his. Whereas my work on Rousseau's *Reveries* is now at an end, my indebtedness to Stanley Cavell is only partially recorded in remarks throughout the text. For I have no doubt that he is present in this book even beyond what I have purposely left implicit, giving me hope that further occasions for manifesting my gratitude will present themselves.

Lindsay Waters has proved to be, once again, a unique editor in his involvement, support, and intense interest in an uncommon project. A year spent at Princeton University has given me the precious time and the perfect environment to complete the writing.

Several friends have read my manuscript, others have been inspiring, supportive, and loving while I was writing it. I single here, among many others, Hagi Kenaan, Ido Geiger, Carolyn Abbate, Lee Mitchell, as well as my parents Hagith and Saul Friedlander.

Reflections of mine often found an echo in Michal Grover-Friedlander's thinking on the apparitions of the operatic voice on screen. Our paths met at times in inspiring conversations, other times almost coincidentally, intimating, in those ways as well, the common ground we have chosen for our dwelling together. I sometimes imagine that our children will pick up this book in the future and enjoy reading it, each in his way. For it is, after all, a book turned with hope to the future. It is to Michal, to Elam, and to Omer, that I dedicate it with love.

Contents

	Introduction: Excessive Measures	1
1	"Here I Am Then"	9
2	From the Nature of Existence to the Existence of Nature	19
3	Space, Time, Motion, and Rest	30
4	A Singular Truth	42
5	The Dimensions of a Place	52
6	Giving Way to Inclination	61
7	Leaves of Memory	75
8	Circles of Destiny	85
9	Exposing Theater	95
10	After Words	106
	Notes	113
	Works Cited	153
	Index	157

No cry of torment can be greater than the cry of one man.
—L. Wittgenstein

Introduction
EXCESSIVE MEASURES

Shortly before his death, David Hume wrote an autobiographical essay he entitled "My Own Life." It opens with the statement: "It is difficult for a man to speak long of himself without vanity; therefore I shall be short."[1] In about ten pages that mostly testify to his sociable nature, Hume recounts "little more than the history of [his] writings." Rousseau's death left his *Reveries of the Solitary Walker* unfinished. This was his third autobiography, after the *Confessions* and the dialogue *Rousseau Judge of Jean-Jacques*. The book opens with the sentence "Here I am then, alone on earth."[2] This difference of temperament—all too painfully manifest in the catastrophic conclusion of the two philosophers' short-lived friendship—can serve to dramatize the question whether philosophy could take the guise of autobiography.

Is autobiography a possible style of philosophy—assuming we are at all prepared to speak of *styles* of philosophy—or is autobiographical writing essentially at odds with the revelation of truth in philosophy? Perhaps its literariness, so often anecdotal in nature, is incompatible with the sober abstractness of philosophical discourse. Or the particularity internal to autobiography might work against the universality of philosophy. Is it, as Hume might say, vanity that clouds truth and makes autobiographical writing inimical to the impartiality of philosophy? Or perhaps, in the end, it is the ordinariness made patent in autobiography that disappoints the wonder expected from philosophical illumination.

These questions should not be settled at the outset, nor, for that matter, answered at the end. Although the present work is an attempt to engage in philosophy by way of reading the autobiographical *Reveries of the Solitary Walker*, the tension in putting those two enterprises together is not eliminated. Balancing the one against the other determined the task of reading: to extend philosophical concepts and reveal the extremities of meaning a life could assume. While such stretching, which is liable to tear apart the fabric of the text, is not usually considered an ideal of reading, it might in the case of the *Reveries* turn out to be a necessity. What follows in this introduction is something of a justification for such excessive measures.

This book grows out of my initial attachment to the *Reveries*. It bears the marks of a childish enthusiasm, an infatuation with a book that seemed to reveal much more than has been recognized about it. It is therefore, above all, a work that is absorbed in the movement of Rousseau's writing, moved by it. Yet it is as easy to respond in cynical disbelief to Rousseau's predicament as it is to identify wholeheartedly with it. The *Reveries* provokes those reactions at every turn, thus showing sympathy and critical distance to be equally misguided, identification posing as great a threat to truthful reading as skeptical aloofness. For the question of distance and intimacy has a much deeper source in the text and would not be solved by too detached or too naïve an approach on the part of the reader. Simply put, the paradox is that Rousseau writes for himself, that the work is not *for us*. That in itself should be enough to disturb any stable identification or fantasized intimacy we could have wished for. It also should forestall the adoption of a critical metaperspective in reading, for the text has anticipated and thus preempted the attempt to keep one's distance. The paradox creates a tension between what is recounted and the conditions of reading that allows no dialectical resolution.

After experiencing that tension, it is hard to know what it would be like to be taken in by the *Reveries,* or to be left out, a distant observer of its happenings. It is hard to gauge Rousseau's tone. Is it as open as it would seem at first? Yet how could it be if Rousseau refuses his words to the reader? But neither is he cagey and secretive. Neither quite hiding, nor revealing anything, what are his ways of concealment and exposure? What is the work's secret, and how does it so often seem able to expose the reader's secrets so well?

In the course of circling around those questions, it becomes clear that they are the very matters to be addressed in reading: that reading itself is the most fundamental issue of the *Reveries.* For whatever else the *Reveries* recounts, they at the same time implicitly address and problematize the intimacy and distance between author and reader, taking you in at the same time as they reject you, being closed by being completely open. One's position in relation to the text—its "I" or its author—is then not to be assumed in advance. A standard to measure one's progress in reading is badly needed, but that standard is, in a reversal typical of the *Reveries,* what only the steps taken in reading can provide.

This book is wholly devoted to the *Reveries* and thus might give the appearance of a straightforward commentary. Each chapter takes its cue from one of Rousseau's walks—and would be read most fruitfully in conjunction with it—accompanying the *Reveries* walk by walk, without quite becoming thereby Rousseau's travel companion. It might appear odd to concentrate so intensely on a single work as if to turn it into a world complete in itself, even more so as the *Reveries* is unfinished. This way of treating a book might seem idealistic, idealizing, or even idolizing. It might seem idealistic insofar as it ignores the material conditions of its production, the state of affairs that gave rise to the writing of the work; idealizing insofar as, focusing on the *Reveries,* it takes into account only Rousseau's picture of himself, his necessarily partial self-image; idolizing insofar as concentrating so intensely on that work leads one to seek a higher meaning in each and every word Rousseau utters.

To clarify my approach, let me say that I aim to raise the question of the form a book could take in philosophy (thus to speculate on what an author and what a reader would be). Isolating the *Reveries* in that way, or making its isolation in reading correspond to the isolation of its author, allows me to think of this book as an idea or a self-contained totality, a world so to speak.[3] Calling the book an idea is to suggest that it allows a movement of meaning revealed in reading beyond the intention of its author. (This would not mean that it is not fully authored, but that the author's genius consists in letting such work take place.)

Thus I want to establish the distinction between the devotion to the *text* of the *Reveries*, which my work intends to exemplify, and the identification with the images that the author has of himself. Reading consists in finding a way to move through the text so as to reach its end and bring it to an end from within, to traverse it and reach a certain stable truth that it opens to. In that sense I can figure my work as a translation of the movement of the *Reveries*. I do not merely follow Rousseau's footsteps in his walks. Neither have I been moved to follow Rousseau's example and write a reverie of my own (although some readers may find my writing affected, more associative than rigorous, fantastic rather than truthful). The notion of translation comes rather to express the idea that the movement internal to the text is followed up; that the text has a life of its own, and its meaning comes to expression in the various media through which it is translated. This movement provides the text with an ever growing circle of meaning, thus intensifying its significance.

The infinitization of the text, a possibility inherent in calling it an idea, becomes the end of reading. But also, in such a condition, the text might appear the object of idolatry, when everything in it scintillates with significance, every term pulling its way, meaningful beyond what anyone could possibly intend. Sometimes, as in my discussion of the first walk, a phrase, even a single word, will arrest the flow of reading. Not only can Rousseau's words bear such an excessive weight, but they *must* so hint, signify beyond what they are usually intended to mean, if reading is to be possible beyond direct communication.

Reading and writing attentive to hints, connections, and affinities of meaning result in significance waxing and waning at every step. But this initial and fleeting sense of the meaning revealed might accurately reflect the instability of significance in ordinary experience. In other words, the peculiar concentration of meaning and the intense and momentary ways in which it appears in the *Reveries* are the upshot of the very relation of autobiography and philosophy formed in that text, of the relation between the ordinary anecdotes of the *Reveries* and their purported higher significance. Rousseau turns to the simple, and his writing remains plain, without thereby being merely the recounting of events. But the higher significance it attains is not figured as a symbol of a philosophical problem. There is no transcendence or sublime redemption of the details of Rousseau's life. They always remain what they are, utterly ordinary and particular, and it is *as such* that they accede to significance.

Writing about the *Reveries* must similarly be attentive to this form of expression and strive to remain always on the same plane while avoiding superficial symbolization. Such writing would steer clear of any separation of higher and lower, of making one thing stand for another, as well as refrain from adopting a unifying external perspective on the text. Writing must reveal relationships along one surface, bring together pieces of Rousseau's autobiography so as to make their philosophical features succinct.

No doubt this way of reading will appear rather strange, a kind of over-reading, finding significance of the highest order in each of Rousseau's often banal anecdotes, willing to read philosophy out of a collection of dried flowers. As if reading itself were affected by Rousseau's excessive assessments of his own state, as he finds persecutory significance in each and every breath his contemporaries emit. In those conditions, what I call the meaning opened by that work might very well appear forced on it, thus raising the suspicion of arbitrariness. Such a danger is addressed by making over-reading a necessity of reading.

The excessive concentration of meaning might be most apparent in the relationships formed between the *Reveries* and other works. For considering the *Reveries* in isolation does not preclude relating it to other writings of Rousseau, or even to those of other philosophers. The question is, rather, what kind of relationships are these, and how they can still be conceived as internal to the work of this text.

A first circle of significance illuminated by the *Reveries* consists of Rousseau's other writings, primarily his major writings on political philosophy, the *Discourse on the Origin of Inequality* and the *Social Contract*. Bringing them into the force field of the *Reveries* is a way of asking about the political stakes of such a solitary work. But this is not achieved by way of contrast or comparison. As a rule I have avoided digressing from the *Reveries* to discuss those other works, but have rather attempted to read them *through* that book, that is, to see how they are refracted in the *Reveries*. This idea of refraction suggests that the *Reveries* can, ideally at least, gather within itself, concentrate, or bring together Rousseau's corpus of writing, recollect what falls under his proper name. This form of reading thus avoids the separation of Rousseau's life work into different periods and sensibilities. It seeks to make further manifest the idea of the book as a concentrated perspective on life, on the world, rather than a partial account of Rousseau's last days that must be balanced against his other works.

Yet what might increase the suspicion of arbitrariness is the way in which I touch upon works of other philosophers to express the meaning of the *Reveries*. In some cases this wider circle of significance will seem more natural than in others. Certain philosophers will be invoked who might have been on Rousseau's mind as he was writing the *Reveries*—particularly Descartes. But throughout I will also be addressing other thinkers whom Rousseau can't possibly have known, for the simple reason that they belong to his posterity. It is customary in discussing a work to look for its antecedents, to appeal to various past sources of influence. But I have chosen mainly to bring in the future, leading all the way to my understanding of the present state of philosophy. Wittgenstein, Heidegger, Benjamin, Cavell, Derrida, and Rawls will appear here, sometimes explicitly, more often between the lines. An initial justification of this anachronistic method, as well as of my attempt to stand at the threshold between the inner space of meaning of the *Reveries* and my sense of the present of philosophy, follows.

So as to avoid psychologizing the issue (as if the important point were how things struck *me*), it must be stressed that the *Reveries* demands a response in writing. Avoiding a detached standpoint or a problematic identification does not require writing an autobiography to match the *Reveries*, but it does require insisting on writing that is cut to your measure, writing you can, if not initially be responsible for, at least assume at the end. Writing out of your experience of philosophy, but more importantly, allowing the writing on that book itself to fashion that experience.[4]

Invoking one's experience of philosophy requires at least assuming and accounting for the particular path it has taken, call it the partiality of one's education. In my case, although this work is turned to Rousseau's *Reveries*, it also opens to the complexities of the present insofar as it engages Stanley Cavell's thinking. His vision of Moral Perfectionism informs my writing and I, in turn, attempt to evoke and address by way of the *Reveries* the Perfectionist concepts of the further self, exemplarity, the ordinary and skepticism, reading and writing, friendship, nature and convention, the affirmation of existence, fate and language.

The detailed juxtaposition of my reading of Rousseau and Perfectionist themes will occur in many remarks in the chapters that follow. But let me say initially that to position Rousseau's work in relation to what Cavell sometimes calls the conversation of Perfectionism is to conceive of the refusal of conversation as itself internal to that outlook. This will demand emphasizing a dimension of the concept of exemplarity which is not so much that of speaking for society, but rather of setting the unchanging standard of nature against society. The Perfectionist outlook will be further inflected insofar as the distance established by Rousseau's refusal of conversation, and the ideal of stability belonging to the standard he sets, must be matched by an account of the nature of Rousseau's writing as well as of the task of reading demanded by the *Reveries*, all of which makes the revelation of truth of this text independent of reaching an understanding with its author.

To clarify this last matter let me add that, while my experience of philosophy certainly influences my reading of the past, and the past in turn fashions that experience, the point is better expressed by saying that conjuring the present space of meaning, concentrating it around the *Reveries*, is itself necessary so as to bring out the truth of that work in reading. The title of my book invokes the notion of afterlife (central to Walter Benjamin's thinking) to point at this co-implication of present and past, of self and other, in coming to terms with the *Reveries*, bringing meaning to an end.[5]

1

"Here I Am Then"

"Here I am then, alone on earth. . ." Dwelling upon this singular beginning, remaining for a while on the threshold of the work, is necessary; such an extremity is not to be glossed over in a premature attempt to understand what lies ahead. The immediate task in confronting the opening phrase is to bring out how strange, how out of the ordinary it is. To make it so striking that its impact resounds and echoes throughout the pages of the book, it is necessary to take the phrase apart, stop the flow of reading, and allow these words to take on the gravity they call for.

To understand the opening of the *Reveries*, it would seem necessary to inquire about its sources, the concrete matters that precipitated Rousseau's catastrophic state, to look for the facts that surround the occasion of writing and explain how he could find himself thus torn away from every attachment. Such a context would no doubt paint a more balanced picture, yet the facts of Rousseau's situation can hardly measure the significance of his composed solitude. Taking them into consideration would only serve to make that opening a disproportionate reaction to certain, admittedly strong, personal enmities, testifying primarily to Rousseau's fragile constitution.

Settling early for the peace of mind required to read the *Reveries* it would be similarly tempting, and just as problematic, to dive into the subjective space of the work, entering Rousseau's state of mind. His opening statement would in that case be assumed to be, strictly speaking, imprecise, deemed by common sense to be a pathological exaggeration, or even a poetic expression of a pathological character, an assumption that would thus draw a further distinction between the real and the literary self.

Such divisions and separations—of the objective, the subjective, and the poetic—are urged to avoid taking Rousseau's words at face value: they would allow addressing the objective conditions of Rousseau's state or his subjective constitution, or simply allow acceptance of the terms of reading, the contract between author and reader that allows entry to the work's world. But what would constitute reading the *Reveries* neither quite as biography, nor simply as a psychological case study, nor yet as literature, but rather as philosophy?

Rousseau does not evince loneliness, he does not merely feel lonely but writes of *being* alone. That latter state commonly depends on delimiting a place in which one is alone (a room, a house). And yet Rousseau writes that he is *alone on earth*, as if he were the only human being on this planet. As he puts it a few pages later, "I live here as in some strange planet on to which I have fallen from the one I knew" (32).[1] Simply alone, Rousseau asserts his solitude. He does not just bemoan being *left* alone, but finds that abandonment affirmable. Assuming his solitude, Rousseau has no one to say "Here I am" *to*, raising the question under what circumstances would he nevertheless utter such a thought. That indexical phrase does not ascertain *where* this takes place, nor *who* I am, leaving existence to be affirmed, making being essentially a matter of being alone (just as Abraham's response "Here I am" to God's call to sacrifice Isaac manifests the deepest existential solitude). A reformulation of that opening sentence, inflecting existence itself with solitude, could be made to say that Rousseau does not feel lonely, nor is he simply left alone, but rather, alone he *is*.

A hint as to how to further read this extreme moment of solitude is provided in Rousseau's use of the word "then" in the middle of the opening sentence. This word seems to point back to what occurred prior to that moment, to the antecedents of the situation he finds himself in. Yet the appearance of the phrase "Here I am then" at the head of the text also suggests something of a beginning. The word "then" would mark a pause, a moment of composure. It would express the amazed realization of finding oneself, from the outset, abruptly thrown in the midst of things, pausing midway, but in an utterly original position.

Letting the word "then" (*donc*) resonate, it echoes with another famous phrase in which that word occurs in transition, as a middle term on the way to existence (or marks existence itself as a middle term, nowhere to be found): "I think therefore I am," whose Latin original, "cogito ergo sum," translates into French as "je pense donc je suis." Starting with Rousseau in the middle of things is turning the "then" that leads on into a "then" that marks a pause. What is supposed to be almost an undecomposable unity, almost not an inference, is here arrested midway, linking thinking to existence by finding rest at the bottom of the abyss.

This association of Rousseau with Descartes makes clear that Rousseau's walk touches upon themes of Descartes' skeptical progress. Rousseau "slipped unwittingly from waking into sleep, or rather from life into death" (27); his waking life assumed the form of his worst nightmare. "Wrenched somehow out of the natural order," he writes, "I have been plunged into an incomprehensible chaos where I can make nothing out" (27). Not knowing any more what to believe, he wishes that this life were only a "bad dream from which I shall wake with my pain gone to find myself once again in the midst of my friends" (27).

The cause of Rousseau's suffering might initially be attributed to his solitude, to the sense of having no contact with another human being. But more precisely, he suffers from his *attachment* to beings with whom no true intimacy is possible. Whereas Descartes primarily doubts his beliefs about the world, Rousseau's anguish concerns his relation to others. "Could I, in my right mind, suppose that I, the very same man who I was then and am still today, would be taken beyond all doubt for a monster, a poisoner, an assassin, that I would become the horror of the human race, the laughing stock of the rabble, that all recognition I would receive from passers-by would be to be spat upon, and that an entire generation would of one accord take pleasure in burying me alive?" (27–28).

Descartes' evil deceiver is for Rousseau transformed into the maddening consciousness that everywhere I am there is an other against me. "I saw that they all without exception remained attached to the most iniquitous and absurd theory that a spirit from Hell could ever have invented" (127). Rousseau, then, is stopped from his spiraling doubt only by being torn away from every human relation. The amazed realization of being utterly alone is both the extremity of the nightmare and opens the possibility of its transfiguration in thinking—it is the turning point of Rousseau's cogito.

To link thinking and existence as Descartes does is to make existence itself something to be recovered, proved in thinking. But for Rousseau it remains open how existence hinges on thinking, for a certain form of thinking is only further disorienting: "the more I think about my present situation, the less I can understand what has become of me" (27). The title of Rousseau's book suggests that existence will be sensed in solitude by his abandoning himself to reverie. But this, in turn, implies that thinking one's way through the doubt does not mean escaping the dream state but rather awakening to it, moving, so to speak, from *rêve* to reverie. In the final account, there will be no recovery, no overcoming of Rousseau's condition, no return to life, but rather the discovery of a state beyond good and evil, finding repose in the midst of persecution. Chaos lingers, yet absolute calm comes to pervade the *Reveries:* "Everything is finished for me on this earth. Neither good nor evil can be done to me by any man. I have nothing left in the world to fear or hope for, and this leaves me in peace at the bottom of the abyss, a poor unfortunate mortal, but as unmoved as God himself" (31). Rousseau's state is utterly and completely hopeless, and only thereby is a different opening to the world possible. Only being dead to the world can give rise to this strange afterlife.

The exceptional situation becomes permanent, if not habitual. Rousseau, living his doubt, outliving himself, writes. And yet the *Reveries* mostly recounts everyday occurrences. Rousseau's autobiographical writing is far from revealing an extraordinary, exceptional life.[2] It is not heroic or particularly virtuous, neither partaking in tremendous historical changes nor eventful in a catastrophic or blissful way, but simply spells out the ordinary internal to any life. This is probably true of all of Rousseau's autobiographical writings, but in the *Reveries* the question is more than ever how is it possible to hold together the catastrophic extreme and the ordinary.[3] How could the ordinary be revealed from within this state of total exclusion? How could the book be true to its opening, sustain such an extremity, without sliding back to normal life?

A temporal solution suggests itself, for the world recovered is a matter of the past. It is primarily in memory, in recollection that the ordinary attains its significance: "Today there is more recollection than creation in the products of my imagination . . . were it not for the hope of a state to which I aspire because I feel it is mine by right, I should now only live in the past" (35). Whereas Descartes mistrusts memory's ability to find the certainty of self-consciousness, Rousseau, closing himself from all that surrounds him, entrusts truth to memory: "Everything external is henceforth foreign to me, I no longer have any neighbours, fellow men or brothers in this world . . . All around me I can recognize nothing but objects which afflict and wound my heart, and I cannot look at anything that is close to me or round about me without discovering some subject for indignant scorn or painful emotion. Let me therefore detach my mind from these afflicting sights; they would only cause me pain, and to no end" (31–32). Seclusion opens up the space of memory in which things attain their true and measured significance. Only in the extreme state does memory truly open up, only against a vision of life in ruins does the ordinary become a measure.

Tracing affinities between Rousseau and Descartes proved fruitful, yet it might lead to consider the *Reveries*, after all, to be not a record of Rousseau's authentic lived experience, but writing more akin to Descartes' methodical path to the cogito—thus to be taken with a grain of salt. Descartes' progress in the *Meditations* does seem at times almost too methodical, too self-possessed, as he resolutely decides to engage in skeptical speculations. This resoluteness might indicate that his doubt should be taken hypothetically, as a controlled thought experiment. Were it truly an ordeal such as the one Rousseau is forced into, it would hardly be undertaken voluntarily.[4]

But just as Descartes might appear too detached, Rousseau often gives the impression of involvement too passionate to be truthful. The apparent excess in his writing, opposed to common sense as it is, raises the question whether it is really possible to speak truthfully (if not ordinarily) of the ordinary in his extreme condition. Wouldn't such isolation and rejection of society make one lose all proportion? Surely some measured restraint is implied by the necessity of addressing another responsibly. And such an address itself would seem the very proof of seriousness, making *writing* in solitude a form of self-deception, even a way of assuring oneself of the presence of another as one fancies being all alone. What does it mean to acknowledge the necessity of address as a condition of seriousness, and at the same time to avoid the dependence implied by taking another into account?

These issues might be addressed by thinking of the conditions of possibility of a truthful philosophical autobiography. Initially, such truthfulness could be identified with the demand to take philosophy upon oneself, embodying it in one's own life. (To be sure, sometimes taking oneself too seriously could lead to confuse embodying thinking and sacrificing one's life to thinking that one thinks.) A first attempt at characterizing the embodiment of thinking through the notion of autobiography would equate truthfulness with the way in which the literary self, the I of the text, remains in accord with the living self (who is, among other things, its author). This may raise various questions, such as the famous and obsessive one whether Rousseau really put his children in an orphanage at birth. It would also situate the reader as a judge of the seriousness of the writing who must check it against the facts and pass moral judgment as to whether Rousseau is true to what he preaches. But Rousseau might neither want nor allow the reader to occupy that position. Indeed, the autobiographical dialogue, *Rousseau, Judge of Jean-Jacques,* leaves no room for such an external standpoint by occupying all the positions in a court of judgment, as well as staging within itself the very division between the living self and the self as it appears through Rousseau's writings.

Too strict an understanding of autobiographical truthfulness as the accord between an empirical and a literary self would further result in the dismissal of any figuration of the self. In particular, if the *Reveries* is the record of Rousseau's reveries, the status of that imaginative production is more at issue than ever. At best, it would require distinguishing fictions that are allowed from those forbidden in a serious autobiography. Although these are surely important issues, they could be resolved only if the preliminary essential question of the place of the figural in language is addressed.

Formulating truthfulness through the adequation of the literary and the living selves would further require considerations external to reading. The living self would be unavailable to reading; it would have to be sought in a factual-historical inquiry. Moreover, the truth about the living self would be the standard for the truthfulness of the literary self. Wanting truthfulness to remain internal to the autobiographical text or to its reading, and the literary self, or its fate in reading, to constitute its standard, would, however, require thinking of the literary self as revealing a truthful option of living beyond one's usual experience of the world. The ordinary self would then be understood not as the result of a factual investigation, identified with the empirical self, but rather as what the literary, higher self must always remain true to, or return to, in order to avoid the danger of fantastic self-empowerment or abstract authenticity. That is to say, the movement between a living and a literary self, marked by a heightened sense of existence, is incorporated into the text. To take as truthful the literary self is to conceive of the text as the field in which that realization of the ordinary can take place. Truthfulness in writing would then depend upon retaining, despite the inevitable tension, both the ordinary and the higher meanings that life can take. It would depend on the writer's being willing to expose himself as thoroughly ordinary and singular at the same time.

These last considerations clarify the most unsatisfactory aspect of the idea of truthfulness as adequation, namely, the inability to account for the dimension of writing itself in its essential relation to life. Whatever else he might have been, Rousseau was a writer and his life was a life of writing. Even more, in the *Reveries* Rousseau abandons everything but writing. Everything revolves around this activity of writing and reading what remains of his life, his reveries: "The free hours of my daily walks have often been filled with delightful contemplations which I am sorry to have forgotten. Such reflections as I have in the future I shall preserve in writing; every time I read them they will recall my original pleasure" (32).

Yet in reading the *Reveries* it is easy to miss the fact that writing itself is Rousseau's foremost concern. He writes about the writing of his reveries: not the experiences or the reveries it triggers, but rather, what it is to recollect them in writing. A working hypothesis of the present reading can be formulated as follows: writing is the fundamental activity in the *Reveries*, and all else, all the other activities Rousseau engages in, are allegories of that writing, and therefore also allegories of reading that text.[5]

Thus the original intuition about truthfulness as adequation is problematized. Writing does not attempt to coordinate thinking with an empirical body; instead, it is writing itself that gives body to thinking. Writing can no longer be conceived as a transition between the living self and the literary self, but becomes the ultimate activity that furthers the *existence* of a self, doubling the self, allowing a further self: "I shall recall in reading them the pleasure I have in writing them and by thus reviving times past I shall as it were double the space of my existence . . . I shall live with my earlier self as I might with a young friend" (34). It is primarily within the field provided by writing that the higher meaning of life can be assessed and realized.

But the task of the revelation of meaning is not solely Rousseau's. Indeed, the higher self is not simply given to reading—it is only the *result* of reading seriously. The seriousness of the writing is not something to ascertain in advance of reading, so as to be assured that it is possible to step into that text. The writer's seriousness is judged by the way his writing allows for serious reading. But consequently it is the reader's seriousness that is put on the line. The higher self of the text is revealed in the movement of reading.

These last considerations raise anew, with full force, the paradox of the *Reveries*, for bringing the reader into the picture in this way seems to fly in the face of Rousseau's self-proclaimed solitude. The *Reveries* would then offer not just Rousseau's private redemption through his resignation to solitude, but set a much more formidable task—to address another person beyond any immediate or mediate communication. Clarifying this point requires a final return to the opening phrase of the *Reveries*. It proved difficult to read this sentence without taking a standpoint that denied its opening terms, either externally by referring to the facts, or internally by diving into the work, wholly identifying with Rousseau's feelings. Remaining at the threshold between the inner and the outer means taking as the most concrete and at the same time the most urgent matter what takes place, so to speak, before one's very eyes—the fact of reading.

The most immediate circle of the work is that of its reader. Yet taking reading itself to be the most concrete context of Rousseau's first sentence has rather strange and alarming consequences. It draws the reader into the current by rejecting him all the more forcefully. Fancying himself to be the addressee of such a work, the reader must face an extraordinary challenge, manifested in the paradox of reading that this work presents. "My enterprise is like Montaigne's, but my motive is entirely different, for he wrote his essays only for others to read, whereas I am writing down my reveries for myself alone" (34). Rousseau's moment of solitude implies that the reader does not exist, making the reading of the *Reveries* impossible from the start, a dead end of reading—unless it just means that the reader needs to transform his thinking in order to become the book's addressee.

A contract which makes reader and author into a society cannot be assumed. But if some meaningful human society is in fact internal to the structure of existence, to Rousseau's cogito, then the generation of a reader must be the *end* of that work. The paradox is that such a society cannot be achieved unless Rousseau abandons the *aim* of reaching the reader. The distance to the other cannot be closed by the author alone; rather, it is up to the reader to reveal the higher self of the text, and thus constitute a meaningful society with the author. Seriousness on Rousseau's part has to do with allowing the reader to bring meaning to an end. Seriousness on the part of the reader would demand fulfilling the meaning of Rousseau's writing without betraying his solitude.

2

From the Nature of Existence to the Existence of Nature

Emerging from the cogito, Descartes repeatedly asks himself *what* is the "I" revealed in that moment. Already in the First Walk Rousseau echoes that question: "But I, detached as I am from them and from the whole world, what am I? This must now be the object of my inquiry" (27). Rousseau finds his essential solitude to be "an exceptional situation . . . certainly worth examining and describing" (33). For his singular exclusion provides access to nature veiled in social existence. The nature of existence reveals for Rousseau the existence of nature. The reveries are the mode of access to that (self) knowledge: "These hours of solitude and meditation are the only ones in the day when I am completely myself and my own master, with nothing to distract or hinder me, the only ones when I can truly say that *I am what nature meant me to be*" (35, my emphasis). Alone on earth, Rousseau returns to the solitude of the state of nature.

Human nature does not shine in the social life Rousseau shies away from. This much could be gleaned from his political writings, especially from the *Discourse on the Origin of Inequality,* which provides the genealogy of society by describing humanity's perfection, which is just as much its decline out of nature. In that *Discourse* Rousseau also warns of the immense difficulties in attempting an investigation of nature. For it is not only the formation of society, but also the very development of human faculties, of imagination, will, thought, and language that conceals nature.

Indeed, the presentation of the state of nature in the *Second Discourse* leaves unclear the very mode of access to such origin. How could Rousseau have knowledge of a state that seems all but nonexistent in the present? Answering that question has taken the form of a reinterpretation of the function of the state of nature. Instead of making it a prehistory of humanity or burying it irretrievably under the rubble of history, Rousseau's state of nature is taken as a graphic representation of essential albeit hidden traits of human nature. The state of nature would further be conceived in relation to a utopia, making it something correlative with an ideal future, as if a well-ordered society originated by way of a fair contract out of the original state.

Rousseau's autobiographical writings, in particular the *Reveries,* allow for a different idea of nature. The opening of the *Confessions* presents nature as ever-present at the limits of society: "I have resolved on an enterprise which has no precedent, and which once complete, will have no imitator. My purpose is to display to my kind a portrait in every way true to nature, and the man I shall portray will be myself" (C, 17). To make this portrait true to nature relates to its inimitability. Nature now shows itself not in the general behavior of mankind but rather in its most singular manifestations. It is no longer recognizable in natural laws governing all, but rather in the exception to the social law, in the unique, in the singular, in that which can only be described in the first person, autobiographically. The most singular becomes the only expression of the natural in an age of universal equalization (which leads not to equality but to conformity). Nature is no distant origin lost in the past, but something that can be revealed here and now. Yet it is present only through the exceptional—that which escapes every common standard. Only in the "strangest situation which any mortal will ever know" can Rousseau be what nature meant him to be. Solitude becomes exception or singularity. In what society has excluded, nature can shine forth. Rousseau recognizes the necessity of exemplifying the exclusion involved in the very formation of society,[1] and takes it upon himself to make manifest the exception in his own person. Writing life as an exception is, first and foremost, writing one's own life. In the *Reveries* that life is no longer to be understood in relation to the forms of life of being in common, in society. It is life severed from common understanding, life permeated by the exception, life in being dead to the world.

Victimization by society as well as expulsion back to nature are ironically depicted in the First Walk by Rousseau's repeated use of the language of the social contract to describe the condition he finds himself in: "The most sociable and loving of men has with a unanimous accord been cast out by all the rest . . . an entire generation, would of one accord take pleasure in burying me alive" (27–28). And being brought back to natural solitude by the excessive persecution of society is what one might, ironically, call being forced to be free.[2]

The peculiar link of the essential and the singular is apparent from the opening sentence of the Second Walk, as Rousseau decides to describe his "habitual state of mind in this, the strangest situation which any mortal will ever know." Yet this opening raises further difficulties as it holds together two opposed concepts: the habitual or ordinary and the strange or singular.

The concept of singularity, it must be stressed, does not mark out the peculiarity of an individual life; it does not mean the person is bizarre, an original, so to speak.[3] It can be compatible with the ordinariness of life if that concept is in turn understood by way of the inner connections of life—the individual life and the world as a whole. The idea of singularity comes to express the connectivity of life to form a world, the possibility of originating the world anew in and with every life; call it the monadic nature of existence. Seen this way the concept of a human life is best characterized as that wherein the world as a whole can be meaningfully refracted. That is, life, that life which is mine, can be viewed as one life among many, but also as an original perspective on the world. Autobiography would, in that case, exemplify the possibility of considering life in its ordinariness as an origin.

To speak of the singularity of the ordinary implies that the ordinary can be experienced as a revelation. This transfigurative dimension of the ordinary is manifest most clearly in the Second Walk, as Rousseau recounts the ecstatic experience of his return to his senses after an accident in which he was knocked unconscious by a giant dog running in front of a carriage:

> [W]hat I felt at that moment was too remarkable to be passed over in silence. Night was coming on. I saw the sky, some stars, and a few leaves. This first sensation was a moment of delight. I was conscious of nothing else. In this instant I was being born again, and it seemed as if all I perceived was filled with my frail existence. Entirely taken up by the present, I could remember nothing; I had no distinct notion of myself as a person, nor had I the least idea of what had just happened to me. I did not know who I was, nor where I was; I felt neither pain, fear, nor anxiety. I watched my blood flowing as I might have watched a stream, without even thinking that the blood had anything to do with me. I felt throughout my whole being such a wonderful calm, that whenever I recall this feeling I can find nothing to compare with it in all the pleasures that stir our lives. (39)

The awakening into the present by way of the accident reaffirms the opening theme of the *Reveries*, namely, that Rousseau is thrown into a state beside himself. He was "wrenched somehow out of the natural order" (27) by the persecution of society, but its excess returns him ecstatically to his world. As with other moments of the *Reveries*, in Rousseau's account of the accident the passivity of suffering is transformed into the repose of abandonment. The accident is the occasion for the ultimate ecstasy—a complete loss of self that allows pure dwelling in the world. Such reversal is characteristic of pivotal moments such as Descartes' cogito, in which utter doubt is converted into the certain knowledge of the existence of the "I." For Rousseau what is accidentally revealed in that reversal is the sentiment of existence.

Early on in the *Discourse on the Origin of Inequality* Rousseau characterizes man in the state of nature through certain sentiments, first and foremost being the sense of his own existence: "His soul, agitated by nothing, is given over to the single feeling of his own present existence" (OI, 46). This sense of existence has been sometimes identified with an instinct of self-preservation, or an indistinct sense of self, making it somewhat inessential for the gist of the *Discourse*. Alternatively, it is conceived negatively, mainly pointing at what man in the state of nature is *not:* he is not yet self-conscious, not yet full of self-love or vanity. This would make that sense of existence something which can hardly be said to be lost in society, or whose loss is entirely inconsequential. Existing unnaturally, one might say, is still existing, whether it is sensed or not.

Yet following the First Walk, reading Rousseau with Descartes, suggests the possibility of identifying the recovery of this sentiment of existence with the affirmation of existence, the appearance of a human subject at the limit of doubt. It characterizes existence as something to be ecstatically discovered or recovered, conceives of the subject as existing in that movement between loss and recovery.

The account of the accident shows that the feeling of existence is not an experience of the *inner self*. Rousseau describes all he perceived as "filled with [his] frail existence." He does not distinguish the *contents* of experience from the *sense* that he has experience, from the reflexive sense of his own existence. Rather, experience *itself* is filled with existence. The ecstasy of existence is being beside oneself, feeling one's existence in all that is habitually thought to be external to the self. In Descartes' cogito, a thinking subject aware of his own existence stands opposed to an external world which that subject must then reach out to. In Rousseau's affective cogito, the existence of the sensuous subject is discovered in the opening to the world.

Rousseau's description relates the renewed belonging to the world with a release to the present, having no past and future. This suggests that the sense of the inner is dependent on a certain schema of inner sense, of time. The preeminent position of the body itself depends on the sense that it houses the inner life, so that when that schema of time is transformed, as he perceives everything to be filled with his frail existence, Rousseau's body finds its place among things, his flowing blood as distant as a stream of water. The disappearance of the inner self does not turn Rousseau into a soulless object among others, but rather the world becomes that body through which the I is revealed.

The ecstatic rebirth into the world is momentary. It is fleeting, transitory, proportionate to the extremity that precipitated it, beyond any capacity of the self to generate it voluntarily. Can this sense of existence, this truthful appropriation of experience, be recreated in a more constructive and lasting form? Could the movement of reverie, tying as it does past, future, and present, allow the release that lets the world meaningfully present itself? This would at least require rethinking the idea of reverie, arguing that, contrary to what is associated with this term, it does not create an inner private space of fantasy, of subjective images and feelings apart from the world, but rather provides a truthful opening to meaning, making it possible for the self to be beside itself.

A related issue arises in trying to understand what it means for Rousseau to *write* recalling an experience so intense and frail. Writing down what seems too much for language itself comes up in another famous instance, recounted in detail in one of his letters to Malesherbes:

> I went to see Diderot, then prisoner at Vincennes. Along the way I started leafing through a *Mercure de France* I had in my pocket. I

stumbled on the question of the Academy of Dijon that gave rise to my first piece of writing. If anything ever resembled a sudden inspiration, it was the movement in me after reading this; suddenly I felt my mind blinded by a thousand lights; a crowd of lively ideas presented themselves to me with a force and confusion that threw me into an inexpressible state of unrest. I felt my head swooning as in a state of drunkenness. A violent palpitation oppressed me, lifting my chest. Unable to breathe while walking, I threw myself under one of the trees of the avenue, and stayed there for half an hour, so agitated that when I finally rose I realized that all the front of my coat was wet with my tears, not even having felt that I shed them. Oh Sir, if I could have written a quarter of what I saw and felt under that tree, with what clarity would I have shown all the contradictions of the social system, with what force would I have exposed all the abuses of our institutions, with what simplicity would I have proved that man is naturally good and that it is only through their institutions that men turn evil. All I could retain of this multitude of great truths, which in a quarter of an hour enlightened me under that tree, is quite feebly dispersed in my three principal writings. (*Oeuvres Complètes*, vol. 1, pp. 1136–37, my translation)

The peculiar method of composition of the *Discourse on the Sciences and the Arts* addresses the problem of being true to such an intense experience:

I composed this essay in a most singular manner, and one which I have almost always followed for my other works. I devoted the night hours to it when I could not sleep. I meditated in bed with closed eyes, and shaped and reshaped my sentences in my head with incredible labour. Then, when I was finally content with them, I committed them to my memory until such time as I could put them on paper. But the break caused by my getting up and dressing made me lose everything, and when I had sat down before my paper hardly a sentence came to me of all those I had composed. It occurred to me, therefore, to take Mme le Vasseur as my secretary. . . . When she arrived I dictated to her from my bed my work of the preceding night; and this method, which I have followed for a long while, has saved for me much that I might otherwise have forgotten. (C, 328)

Rousseau connects the process of writing from memory and the problem of remembering dreams (as though composing in bed instead of sleeping were similar to dreaming). The lapse of memory caused by getting up and dressing is familiar when it comes to remembering dreams. Rousseau commits his sentences to memory before writing them down. Thus in a reversal of the usual process in which what is written can then be learned by heart, writing itself records what is memorable.

The *Reveries* raises even more acutely the question of what it is to commit memory to writing and to have a writing that is committed to memory: "The free hours of my daily walks have often been filled with delightful contemplations which I am sorry to have forgotten. Such reflections as I have in the future I shall preserve in writing. Every time I read them they will recall my original pleasure" (32). The state of reverie often involves a spontaneous mental movement, essentially fluid, smooth, and lyrical. It seems opposed to writing, which may appear more rigid, arbitrary, external, or conventional. A reverie is moreover a distracted state opposed to the concentration demanded by writing. Writing cannot occur at the same time as reverie. But even if one conceives of writing as recalling the reverie after the fact, in a more sober mood, remembering or attending to it in memory, the problem is that one tends to forget reveries: "if we completely ceased to experience it, we should soon lose all knowledge of it" (36). Even worse, as Rousseau is the first to admit, truly remembering a reverie means reentering its mood. Instead of writing one relives that state: "As I tried to recall so many sweet reveries, I relived them instead of describing them. The memory of this state is enough to bring it back to life"(36).

Is Rousseau in the *Reveries* trying to evoke the mood of a reverie and in so doing to produce writing that effaces itself (just as the book itself would attempt to efface the fact that writing has an addressee)? Is he creating the illusion of listening to the sound of the soul itself, recovering by means of the poor substitute of writing a plenitude beyond language itself? Rousseau's description suggests another function for writing: "I shall recall in reading them the pleasure I have in writing them and by thus reviving times past I shall, as it were, double the space of my existence. In spite of men I shall still enjoy the charms of company, and in my decrepitude I shall live with my earlier self as I might with a younger friend" (34). To have the pleasure of one's own company is not merely to enjoy being alone, but also to be able to be an other to oneself. Befriending oneself would demand making the self other to itself, by faithfully recollecting the past so as to prepare small presents for the further self. But this very capacity for self-reliance depends on the reveries being written. Indeed, it is only in the externality and independence of writing that there is in that self-relation another to befriend.

Truthfully returning to a reverie does not involve a faithful correspondence to a past state of affairs, but rather a sort of re-creation, allowing again the freedom of movement. Recalling the reverie is calling it forth, regenerating meaning. Similarly, writing is opening thought rather than attempting to adequately represent it. The reading of the *Reveries* does produce a very peculiar movement of thought in the reader. Instead of recalling Rousseau's reveries, the work opens the space for the reader's relation to the text. It makes the *Reveries* into the opening of an expanse in which the reader can relate to that work thoughtfully.[4]

After the accident, a rumor had spread that Rousseau died of its consequences and so he, still alive, was given a glimpse of the world after his death. The account of that bizarre occurrence explains Rousseau's sense that, as he writes in the First Walk, "an entire generation would of one accord take pleasure in burying me alive" (28).[5] What emerges in the peace that follows the accident is the uncanny realization that Rousseau accepts the fate imposed on him. He is lingering beyond the limits of life, in a limbo between his death to the world and the demise of his body.

Rousseau's realization of his existence in this ghostly state, between two deaths, crucially inflects for him the problem of writing.[6] Indeed, as a consequence of the accident Rousseau discovers that his enemies were preparing fake works under his name to be printed after his death: "I can have no chance," he writes, "of handing on anything precious to future ages without passing through hands that have an interest in suppressing it" (44). This gives a clearer sense of Rousseau's victimization. His identity is fabricated, the words he utters are twisted and changed to such an extent that he can no longer recognize himself in them. Such a sense of persecution is not just the result of, literally, attempts to forge works that would be attributed to him; it arises from the very difficulty of controlling meaning. It concerns the fate of the writings left after death, the afterlife of Rousseau's writings.[7]

If the *Reveries* is an answer to this predicament, then Rousseau must write while taking into account the fate of his writings—as it were, while living his own afterlife. There are two ways in which it is possible to conceive of the work as an answer to Rousseau's condition. First, the text is written solely for the benefit of its author. It provides Rousseau with a pleasure that depends on his capacity, when dead to the world, to use his own past fund of life, feed on his own substance. This would reinforce the picture of Rousseau as ultimately craving the immediacy of self-presence and closing himself from all. The drawback of such an interpretation is that it cannot account for the reader. Rousseau would close himself off from everyone, write only for himself, and thus make anyone who reads him a *voyeur* attempting to steal pleasure at a distance.

Alternatively, one could think of this text as assuming a reader without addressing him. That is, the reader must come to the text on his own, or better still come to his own, by way of reading the text. Rousseau writes *for* no one. It is not necessary to believe that the author engages in the nostalgic fantasy of finding a reader who will truly understand him, only that he writes knowing that meaning has a life and a death of its own.[8] This leads to a different understanding of the ghostly position of Rousseau, haunting the world. For the drastic state of being already "dead to the world" is not just a description of the individual's fate, it must also be a characteristic of meaning itself, of language. The aftermath of the accident shows something essential to meaning itself, that it can be expressed beyond the intention of its author, beyond its original life. Rousseau needs to leap over and beyond his generation, or more precisely, since each generation is bound to the next in chains of public opinion, it is the necessity of introducing a break in time so as to give birth to the generation that will find what he abandons (without thereby bringing him back to life). But to create such a break is precisely to allow meaning to remain beyond the continuity provided by intentional communication.

The point can be made slightly differently, thinking again in terms of Rousseau's description of the awakening after the accident, of that experience which touches upon the limits of experience itself: the disappearance of the inner self and the rebirth into existence in the world. Rousseau's writing as a whole must similarly provide a truthful opening to meaning. For that to be the case, the interiority of this text itself has to be breached. But this breach is the reader's to make. That is, it is necessary to read through the *Reveries* in such a way that meaning is brought to an end, thus fragmenting the inner unity of the book. Any chance of identifying with Rousseau in the process would be lost, but it might precisely answer the paradox of the work, provide a way to read him so as to acknowledge his irretrievable distance.

3

Space, Time, Motion, and Rest

Rousseau's account of his accident underscores a theme present throughout the *Reveries*. At the limit, an affective transformation takes place, and anxious victimization gives way to an ecstatic sense of security or repose. Just as Rousseau's doubt is to be read as taking up Descartes' skeptical progress leading to the cogito, so too his affective transformation should be understood as providing insight into the human constitution, raising the question of what it is for an affect to be conceived ontologically rather than psychologically.

In this connection one should note that Descartes' *Second Meditation* keeps going over the question of what the "I" is that has just been discovered. Such repetition is symptomatic of an instability, as if every time Descartes stepped away from the certainty of the cogito, trying to build upon it and put some substance around this hinge which is the "I," he is returned to it, reminded of that pivotal moment. Discovering the "I," Descartes inadvertently reveals the ghostly nature of spirit that requires constant summoning lest it disappear.

The repose, the peace of mind associated with the sentiment of existence, appears to be achieved lastingly for Rousseau only in putting thinking in motion. No substance is discovered in Rousseau's cogito, but rather a transformation, a transitional state, a motion in which existence is revealed. He will find existence in movement, in the reverie or in the walk, as if doubling the self—not by separating mind and body, but by opening the space of memory in which the recognition of meaning takes place. This movement allows Rousseau to think of what is moving or affecting in the cogito: to speak of a *feeling* of existence.

Feeling the movement of the mind itself, Rousseau echoes what could be called the affirmative moment implicit in Descartes' cogito: the possibility of transforming utmost doubt into absolute certainty is contingent on the emptiness of the cogito, on its being purely reflexive thinking, affirmed over and above all contents of thought. For Rousseau even the most dejected state is capable, in and through the return of reverie, of affirmation. The very fact of thinking allows him to stand, so to speak, beyond good and evil, making the discovery of nature something of a reversion to a state of creation. The *Reveries* as a whole is an account of that transformation of experience in memory, making it affirmable beyond the pleasures or pains usually associated with it. As was evident in the account of the accident, existence is felt in having experience at all. Similarly, one could say that the pleasure in the reverie is not dependent on its content, but on the movement of the mind itself. Only insofar as pleasure is taken in the very opening of meaning can it be de-psychologized, severed from any interest, desire, or aim.

To further characterize that movement, consider that whereas Descartes writes meditations, Rousseau writes reveries. The meditations are structured so as to separate day and night, establishing a day-by-day progress, allowing for rest after each day's effort of thought so as to recreate a world after six such days. Importantly, there are only six meditations, identifying them with the days of work, leaving out the seventh day of rest. Can work or the labor of thought, day after day, recreate a world? Or to further pursue the analogy, the seventh day of rest might contribute just as much to the sense of the world as the six days that preceded it. Is there, indeed a connection between the sense of createdness and repose?

And if so, what is the motion of thinking that reveals rest, that does not advance but allows one to dwell in place?

Although the progress of the *Meditations* takes place day by day with a night's rest between each, at the end of the first day Descartes blurs the clean division of day and night, dream and wakefulness:

> But this is an arduous undertaking, and a kind of laziness brings me back to normal life. I am like a prisoner who is enjoying an imaginary freedom while asleep; as he begins to suspect that he is asleep, he dreads being woken up, and goes along with the pleasant illusion as long as he can. In the same way, I happily slide back into my old opinions and dread being shaken out of them, for fear that my peaceful sleep may be followed by hard labour when I wake, and that I shall have to toil not in the light, but amid the inextricable darkness of the problems I have now raised. (*Meditations*, p. 15)

This twilight time between wakefulness and sleep seems to be shaken off by the cogito and does not recur in the later transitions from day to day, although Descartes still worries about his "tendency to hang on to long-held beliefs" that "cannot be put aside so quickly." What might even be more worrisome is that, despite the cogito, or even *because* of it, a sense of unreality comes to pervade everyday existence. The cogito might be said to recreate doubt, or retrospectively validate the doubt leading to it. Coming out of the ecstasy of the moment, Descartes might find that the whole world had been thrown into doubt more certainly than he could ever have dreamt to achieve methodically. On the downward skeptical path, Descartes unburdens himself of his previous beliefs with the hope of discovering a new world. Emerging out of the cogito, he must recover the only world there is, have it live up to his new knowledge. But *because* of the knowledge he has achieved, it is liable to appear to him now, more than ever, a world of somnambulists. Living in it would be like "being a prisoner enjoying an imaginary freedom while asleep."

In order to shake off the dream, to return to the world with eyes wide open and maintain the wakefulness of the revelatory moment of certainty, Descartes might require the assurance of a benevolent creator. He might also need to sharply separate the knowledge he gains from the everyday experience he leaves behind. But he also needs to construe his own thinking as *work*. Such a gradual reconstruction of the world is the best defense against chaos. Thus something of the clean division between day and night, days of work and days of rest, must be recovered as Descartes builds upon the secure ground of the cogito.

Rousseau's affirmation of the world depends on the world itself being filled with his existence, experiencing the day-to-day as if it were creation itself. This would mean avoiding the sharp separation of the ecstatic cogito from the arduous labor that reconstructs a world on solid foundations. But it would further require an acknowledgment of the continuous presence of doubt, thus the necessity of repeating the cogito, finding rest only at the bottom of the abyss. Rousseau cannot stop to impress his new knowledge on his memory, as Descartes did at the end of the second meditation. Rather, it is the movement of memory itself, the constant recalling and return, that is required to bring about the truthful appropriation of experience.

Rousseau's *Reveries* brings together day and night in the state of mind of daydreaming, making each moment of thought be of what is passing. The reveries are not ordered according to any clear method: "These pages will be no more than a formless record of my reveries. . . . I shall say what I have thought just as it came to me, *with as little connection as the thoughts of this morning have with those of last night*" (32, my emphasis). If thinking is an arduous effort for Descartes, for Rousseau the reverie is from the start recreation: "Sometimes I have thought quite profoundly, but this has rarely given me any pleasure and has almost always been done against my will and under duress as it were; reverie amuses and distracts me, thought wearies and depresses me; thinking has always been for me a disagreeable and thankless occupation. Sometimes my reveries end in meditation, but more often my meditations end in reverie" (107). This contrast between work and recreation is complex. Above all, Rousseau's state of restfulness should not be construed as escapism. The release from the realm of work characterizes a new mode of thinking, of attunement with the world. That release is not an escape from the tension of existence but rather the discovery of a resting place in the midst of doubt. It is not an attempt to avoid the toil internal to life, but the attainment of a deeper repose, at the limits of life, which bespeaks of unconditioned, complete, and irrevocable abandonment.

Assessing motion and rest demands relating time and space. Descartes' cogito happens in the blink of an eye, without time interposing itself. It is a momentous and momentary discovery. Not only is it an isolated act of thinking, it also isolates thinking from the whole extent of life. Despite the autobiographical tone of the opening of the *Meditations* and the intrinsic necessity of stating the cogito in the first person singular, Descartes avoids linking autobiography to the proof of existence. For memory is doubtful, and past convictions ought to be rejected so as to achieve the certainty of the "I think." That act of thinking is not to be repeated along life's way, reaffirming existence. It provides a foundation to be uncovered once in a lifetime that will henceforth lie hidden under the edifice of knowledge.

If the awakening from the accident is for Rousseau the paradigm for a heightening of experience, then clearly the present is of fundamental importance. But even in that critical moment the other dimensions of time come into play, albeit negatively, in his having no awareness of past or future. The temporal synthesis is even more pronounced when considering the recovery of experience in reverie. Reverie is indeed a state characterized by a peculiar temporality. The past is the material of the reverie. But while the thinking that proves existence is essentially a work of remembering, the temporality of the reveries involves no less the future, for it is only by extinguishing all hope that Rousseau can be released to the absolute security of the present by way of his devoted appropriation of the past.

Not only is time refigured in Rousseau's confrontation with Descartes, but also extension—space or the sense of place. Indeed, one of the things to emerge from Rousseau's account of the accident is that existence is sensed in the attunement to the surrounding world. A strange reversal of the cogito takes place insofar as the disappearance of the self, interpreted through the idea of the inner, is the condition of the assumption of subjectivity. The soul is not separable from its world, even in the extreme condition that opens the *Reveries*. To make the point succinct, it is possible to rewrite the opening phrase as "Here I am then alone-on-earth." Contrary to Descartes' cogito, the world does not disappear in that utmost solitude of the self, but rather the inner relation between soul and world is revealed.

Rousseau hints at his odd conception of the soul in the title of his work, as he relates the wandering of the mind to the vagabonding of the body. But rather than form a parallel between two realms, he points to the concreteness of reverie. The imagination always requires some sensuous matter to rework, even to figure thought itself. Walking, preeminently, is such a figure of thought. Descartes' division of the human into the thinking substance and the extended substance is translated into the difference between two ways of being in the world; the passage between those two modes of existence can be called "attaining intelligibility." Rousseau advances to the discovery of the thoughtful subject from the condition of a ghost haunting a world unintelligible to him. He realizes the soul's originary affinity with its world. It is in recovering the world in memory, realizing its meaning, that the "I" secures its unique existence. One might also say that Rousseau's singular character emerges by reworking, in the space of memory, his experience into a world, his thoughtfulness manifest in the way his life provides a singular perspective of the world as whole.

To further establish the affinity of self and world, consider that reverie, first and foremost, induces a mood. Its affective dimension cannot be identified with a feeling of pleasure caused by this or that thing, nor is it the result of achieving one aim or another. That this state can be experienced as revelatory derives primarily from the fact that it constitutes no concerted effort of thinking about anything. This thinking is concrete, yet holds to nothing in particular. The movement of the reverie reveals the surroundings of thinking, for it is not a state of mind that is directed, reaching at, or grasping this or that thing. Rather, it is a self-sustaining wandering of the soul which reveals the subject in its potentiality and the world as the place in which that freedom takes effect.[1]

This quality of the reverie is the basis for the image of the barometer through which Rousseau characterizes his investigation, suggesting that the soul pervades its surroundings like air:

> I ought to proceed with order and method, but such an undertaking is beyond me, and indeed it would divert me from my true aim, which is to give an account of the successive variations of my soul. I shall perform upon myself the sort of operation that physicists conduct upon the air in order to discover its daily fluctuations. I shall take the barometer reading of my soul, and by doing this accurately and repeatedly I would perhaps obtain results as reliable as theirs. However, my aim is not so ambitious. I shall content myself with keeping a record of my readings without trying to reduce them to a system. (33)

The formless record of the *Reveries*, then, is not merely opposed to Descartes' orderly and methodical inquiry that puts together one day after another. It also sets an opposition between establishing knowledge based on first principles and discovering the soul by way of its world. Existence is not a matter of knowledge, it is sensed in the return to the self that opens to the world. And the world is not an object of knowledge to be reconstructed step by step, methodically, by way of its facts or things. Knowledge requires method, but it is necessary to find ways in the world, to make one's way in it. This in turn requires orientation apart from a goal, a *sense* of one's surroundings. Since the fundamental figure for thinking in the *Reveries* is walking, walking should not be thematized as taking steps to reach some point. Rather, walking constantly covers the same expanse, remaining always in the same domain. Indeed, this is why the sense of the world as a resting place can only be achieved in movement.

Rousseau's Third Walk moves between the ages of life, relating them to the time of thinking. Both Rousseau and Descartes describe a disquiet that has to do with experiences of childhood. Descartes writes: "Some years ago I was struck by the large number of falsehoods that I had accepted as true in my childhood, and by the highly doubtful nature of the whole edifice that I had subsequently based on them."[2] Rousseau echoes that description:

> Thrown into the whirlpool of life while still a child, I learned from early experience that I was not made for this world, and that in it I would never attain the state to which my heart aspired. Ceasing therefore to seek among men the happiness which I felt I could never find there, my ardent imagination learned to leap over the boundaries of a life which was as yet hardly begun, as if it were flying over an alien land in search of a fixed and stable resting place. (48)

Whereas for Descartes childhood is the age in which one most unreflectively accepts falsehoods, and the resolutions of adulthood are ways of correcting those mistakes, Rousseau describes his resolutions of maturity as being *faithful* to childhood.[3]

Childhood is problematized by Rousseau, with his sense of being thrown into life, needing to leap out toward a distant future. Taking adulthood to be determined by this sense of childhood would thus mean thinking of it as addressing the problem of entering a world. Relating this sense of thrownness to Heidegger's use of the term underscores the fact that the child comes into an existing world and language, and that to be a child is to face this essential belatedness that is constitutive of human nature. Such a sense of being thrown can lead to flight, to a fall, that is, to a defensive adoption of the images offered to form one's identity.

Remaining faithful to childhood, therefore, means resisting those models of identification and constantly thinking in terms of the thrownness of existence, seeking the leap that provides repose. Elaborating on the account of the accident, one might say that entering a world by being thrown into it makes the recovery of a transformed world something that is impossible to achieve step by step. It is a matter of leaping or of release; one more way to complicate the pace of Rousseau's walks.

Both Descartes and Rousseau consider the end of their thinking to be stability, but in Descartes' account this stability is meant to provide the ground upon which to construct the edifice of science. The stable ground is to function as a foundation for construction. Rousseau, meanwhile, thinks of stability as a resting place that allows him to give up every project, "making no further effort to climb up of whatever situation I was in and of spending the rest of my life living from day to day with no thought of the future" (50–51). To rest is to reach a place that allows you to do nothing, where the soul can feel at home or find peace.

It is significant that the walk is that resting place for Rousseau, emphasizing that the abode of the soul is not to be thought of as something that needs to be *constructed*, but rather as taking place in the open, as a sense of the open. Rousseau aims to find rest in the midst of movement. That is, he recognizes the problem of existence in time and the necessity for repose to take that movement into account.

Descartes finds himself writing meditations in midlife, at the height of his powers. He decides to engage in this enterprise when he is most ready for it.

> I realized that it was necessary, once in the course of my life, to demolish everything completely and start again right from the foundations if I wanted to establish anything at all in the sciences that was stable and likely to last. But the task looked an enormous one, and I began to wait until I should reach a mature enough age to ensure that no subsequent time of life would be more suitable for tackling such inquiries. This led me to put the project off for so long that I would now be to blame if by pondering over it any further I wasted the time still left for carrying it.[4]

In the Third Walk, Rousseau recounts an earlier attempt, at midlife, when he felt fully mature, to face the problem of time, by renouncing any ambition or project and fixing his opinions once and for all on what was essential. In a language that cannot fail to recall Descartes' resolution, Rousseau describes his own determination:

> I said to myself:. . . Let me seek [my philosophy] with all my might while there is still time, so that I may have an assured rule of conduct for the rest of my days. I am now in the prime of life and the fullness of my mental powers. I am about to enter my decline. If I wait any longer, I shall no longer have all my powers to devote to my tardy deliberations . . . Let me decide my opinions and principles once and for all, and then let me remain for the rest of my life what mature consideration tells me I should be. (53)[5]

In contrast to Descartes, Rousseau's midlife attempt to fix his opinions proves, at the end, not sufficient to face doubt. As the opening of the *Reveries* makes manifest, it is only the solitude of reverie that offers him the ultimate resting place. Deciding his opinions and principles nevertheless provides resources against adversity, and allows him to abandon himself wholly to what pleases him most, the reveries.

Reminding himself, late in life, of his attempt to decide once and for all on all matters of importance, Rousseau, "sunk in mental lethargy," retains no more justifications for his conclusions, nor has he any memory of the arguments that supported his position and led him to adopt his principles. It is as though the principles he chose were in themselves less important than the fact that he opted for them, when he was most mature and balanced to take a decision. It is the memory of the seriousness of his past efforts that provides all the necessary justification. New arguments and doctrines arise, new objections which Rousseau is totally unable to counter: "being incapable of the thought processes which would be necessary to reassure myself, I feel the need to recall my former conclusions; I remember the painstaking attention and sincerity of heart which led me to them and all my confidence returns" (61).

Rousseau would seem to advocate a dogmatic position, closing himself from any new argument. But it is more accurate to say that he recognizes the finitude of human knowledge: "I knew when I was pondering these things, that the human understanding, limited by the senses, could not fully comprehend them" (59). Rousseau recognizes the dialectical nature of all attempts to achieve absolute knowledge, finding "objections which I could not resolve, but which were met by equally powerful objections in the opposite system" (55). He is drawing a distinction between reasoning and reason, between matters of knowledge in which there are *sides* to take and the virtues of steadfast devotion, memory, and faithfulness which are absolute and make manifest the relation of the self to the world, or to life as a whole.

The time of thinking in the *Reveries* is no longer, as in Descartes' *Meditations,* the maturity of midlife. Philosophy comes too late, when nothing more can be done. Not the resolution and decisiveness of maturity, but abandonment governs thinking and writing: "We enter the race when we are born and we leave it when we die. Why learn to drive your chariot better when you are close to the finishing post? All you have to consider then is how to make your exit. If an old man has something to learn, it is the art of dying, and this is precisely what occupies people least at my age; we think of anything rather than that." (48)[6]

Rousseau writes in a deeply melancholic state: "My fellow men might return to me but I should no longer be there to meet them (. . .) it is too late" (30). He has no hope of being revived in reading, but writes nevertheless. Does that mean that it is too late for everything but for writing? More accurately, the question is, what is writing that comes too late, abandoned writing beyond expectation?

4

A Singular Truth

The Fourth Walk is probably the closest to a sustained meditation of all the walks in Rousseau's *Reveries,* its object being the nature of lying and truth-telling. The meditation is triggered by the coincidence of reading an essay by Plutarch entitled "How a Man May Profit by His Enemies" and coming across a piece of writing by Abbé Rozier dedicated to Rousseau in the words: "*Vitam vero impendenti*—Rozier" ("To devote one's life to the truth"). Rousseau reads sarcasm in that dedication and places Rozier in the ranks of his persecutors, whose every word chagrins him. But at the same time Rozier precipitates the meditation from which Rousseau can profit. The reading and the dedication of the writing become related, and the title of Plutarch's essay provides a characterization of the condition Rousseau finds himself in: "The moments of rapture and ecstasy which I sometimes experienced during these solitary walks were joys I owed to my persecutors; without them I should never have known or discovered the treasures that lay within me" (36).

Rozier's dedication repeats the motto Rousseau chose for himself, so it is not in and of itself offensive.[1] What makes the difference is that the restatement is not an homage, but an ironic duplication that casts doubt on the intention of the one who swears to that principle. For one cannot say to another person, "Devote your life to the truth!" (just as "Know thyself" is something that could, at most, be inscribed on the temple of a god; from the mouth of another person it would sound condescending). Some things are not sayable to another, or when said, are bound to sound either ironic or moralizing. But then, under what conditions can I say something to myself that would commit me rather than turn my words into a private language? Conversely, what are things that ought to be said—that are owed—to another?

The question of dedicating one's life to the truth arises on the occasion of the dedication of a piece of writing, but it is just as much an issue of the dedication *to* writing (as well as devotion to reading, since it arises in reading Plutarch. This, Rousseau notes, "was my first childhood reading and he will be the last reading of my old age" [63].) In particular, it arises in relation to Rousseau's own work, for the motto "to dedicate one's life to the truth" can name the autobiographical quest: not only to pursue truth, but to give it a body, or lend it a tongue through writing one's life. Rozier uses that dedication sarcastically, but in so doing raises for Rousseau the question of what it means to put his own writing under the sign of the same dedication. Is dedication to truth an *obligation* to be truthful, stated in writing? Or is it something that cannot be said, but must be shown *through* what one writes? And how is one a devoted reader of such dedicated writing?

Rousseau decides to devote his walk of the following day to self-examination on such weighty matters. As he sets out to put his resolution into practice, he recalls a "terrible lie" he told in his youth, "the memory of which has troubled me all my life and even now, in my old age, adds sorrow to a heart already suffering in many ways." The incident is recounted in detail in the *Confessions*. While in the service of Mme de Vercellis, he steals an old pink and silver ribbon. Found in his possession, he claims it to be a present he received from his fellow servant, Marion. Thus accusing Marion, Rousseau further shames her by implying that she attempted to seduce him. When confronted by the Count, in Marion's presence, Rousseau repeats his story. The Count dismisses them both, saying that "the guilty one's conscience would amply avenge the innocent." Rousseau adds: "His prediction was not wide off the mark. Not a day passes on which it is not fulfilled" (C, 87).

The memory of the lie does not disappear with time, and it comes to haunt Rousseau in the most varied circumstances. He finds the world closing on him, seeming to fill up with persecutions that present themselves to him as the avenging of poor Marion. Rousseau never settles accounts with the real victim, but as atonement for his sin he brings up his "forty years of honest and upright behavior," as well as the suffering inflicted by Marion's "many avengers in this world."

Rousseau also presents the lie as a central reason for writing his *Confessions*, making it an exemplary instance of writing in the form of a confession. He writes the episode as if confessing to it for the first time ever, hoping thereby to relieve his conscience from the burden of that memory which refuses to disappear. Book Two of the *Confessions* ends with an avowed hope: "This is all I have to say on the subject. May I never have to speak of it again" (C, 89). And yet, as is evident from the Fourth Walk, the haunting memory returns, despite everything, its persecutory force undiminished, threatening to disturb the peacefulness in reverie. That repetition points also to the failure of the confession as a mode of revelation of truth. Indeed, it might precisely show that writing in a confessional mode partakes of the guilt of the original sin. It raises the question whether the writing of the confession is not merely a substitute for moral action, a way for Rousseau to excuse himself, to avoid responsibility, thus recreating guilt instead of atoning for the deed.[2]

In order to understand the shift that takes place in the *Reveries*, consider that in a confession truth appears not merely as the correct accounting of some state of affairs, but also as addressed to another. It is, moreover, speech that is *owed* to another, a matter of justice (though the addressee of the speech act is not necessarily the one to whom truth is owed). The devotion to truth as justice is the fundamental virtue that Rousseau attributes to "the true man": "For a man of this kind, justice and truth are synonyms which can be used interchangeably. The holy truth which his heart worships does not consist of trivial facts and unnecessary names, but of faithfully giving every man his due in matters which really concern him, whether it be good or evil, reputation, honor or dishonor, praise or blame" (72).

The exemplification of truth in Rousseau's *Reveries of the Solitary Walker* no longer fits the model of the intimacy between truth and justice. It is dedication to truth in isolation, released from what is owed to another (or to oneself): "These pages may therefore be regarded as an appendix to my *Confessions*, but I do not give them this title, for I no longer feel that I have anything to say that could justify it . . . I have no more reason to praise than to condemn myself: henceforward I am of no importance among men, and this is unavoidable since I no longer have any real relationship or true companionship with them" (33).

That release raises the question whether there is language beyond the *obligation* of truth, but not beyond truthfulness. Related to that is a serious obstacle that stands in the way of calling the *Reveries* truthful. A reverie is the product of unbridled imagination and memory. If the *Reveries* is the consequence of such a movement of the mind, it would seem to bring the text closer to the status of fiction. Tying together truth and justice allowed Rousseau to distinguish fiction and lie: "To lie without advantage or disadvantage to oneself or others is not to lie; it is not falsehood but fiction" (69). Since Rousseau owes nothing to anyone, his imaginative writing is no lie. But can the idea of writing not owed to anyone allow for a (no doubt unintuitive) category of truthful fiction?

Just as the nature of devotion to truth (if not the obligation to it) needs to be considered, so do the motives for lying. In the *Reveries* as in the *Confessions*, the predominant motive is shame, and overcoming it is necessary for truthfulness: "I do not lie out of personal interest or self-love, still less out of envy or malice, but simply out of embarrassment and false shame" (74). And in the *Confessions* he all but points to the motive of his action as shame of his desire for Marion.

> Never was deliberate wickedness further from my intention than at that cruel moment. When I accused that poor girl, it is strange but true that my friendship for her was the cause. She was present in my thoughts, and I threw the blame on the first person who occurred to me. I accused her of having done what I intended to do myself.... my invincible sense of shame prevailed over everything. It was my shame that made me impudent, and the more wickedly I behaved the bolder my fear of confession made me. (C, 88)

Finding the source of the misdeed in shame rather than evil intention facilitates the exculpation from it. That is, the motive of shame allows Rousseau to acknowledge the evil deed while insisting on his essentially good character. It is further understandable that Rousseau has thought of confession as the mode in which truth can shine forth out of his struggle to overcome his "innate timidity." For a confession does not merely reveal the factual truth, but in being addressed to an other, it exposes the self to the shame that was at the source of lying.

Yet shame is problematic in being reactive, usually shame *from* another. Thus even its overcoming would still leave one involved with others, precisely by struggling to get free of them. To be true to Rousseau's utter abandonment in the *Reveries*, another idea of exposure and the overcoming of shame is required. Throughout his works Rousseau writes so as to escape the dependence on the gaze of another, writes beyond the expectations and interests of a human other. Recreating the intimacy of a situation of confession might be one such device, but the radical solution he presents in the *Reveries* involves writing that is exposed but not given to a human gaze. The shame to be overcome is shame *in oneself,* but not *from another.* It is, one might say, shame in showing human nature by way of exposing one's ordinary partiality. Indeed, even in the *Confessions* Rousseau distinguishes the sense of confessing one's sins to another and the ideal of doing justice to *human nature.* This latter notion demands truth to be revealed beyond good and evil, making innocence a return to the state of creation. Further, it is no exposure to a human other but to a divine gaze: "I have displayed myself as I was, as vile and despicable when my behavior was such, as good, generous and noble when I was so. I have bared my secret soul as Thou thyself hast seen it, Eternal Being!"

The *Reveries* is more radical insofar as it is writing itself that must be left exposed, turning the exposure of meaning into an exposure *to* meaning. Rousseau forms such a connection between shame and the excess of meaning:

> I have often lied out of shame, to avoid embarrassment in trivial affairs or affairs that concerned only me, as when in order to keep a conversation going I have been forced by the slowness of my ideas and my lack of small talk to have recourse to fiction for something to say. . . . The talk runs on more quickly than my ideas and forces me to speak before thinking, so that I have often been led into foolish and inept statements, which my reason had condemned and my heart disowned before I had finished speaking, but which had forestalled my judgement and thus escaped its censure. (74)

Rousseau suggests that he conceals himself in fiction because of a difficulty he has in keeping up with meaning, a lack of presence of mind. Although here he addresses the problem of exposure to another and shame from another, it is possible to ask whether there is not also an excess of meaning internal to language itself. To face this predicament, to be truthful in the face of such excess, would demand in the first place letting yourself be exposed to it, rather than attempting to simulate presence of mind by means of fictions. Thus a clear distinction appears between confession and exposure. For in the idea of confession a purity of heart, of intention, is essential, whereas the exposure to meaning requires precisely giving up intention, withstanding the excess.

But what kind of movement of meaning would constitute the acceptance of that exposure? The literal knows of no excess, and fictions simulate presence of mind. Are there figures of the imagination that are truthful from the start? Such issues may find answers in Rousseau's fable of the origin of language. A fable is not a historical hypothesis about origins; rather, it serves to present, mythically or figuratively, dimensions of language which might not be readily apparent. This does not mean that such a presentation is not truthful. But it is nevertheless a mythical presentation of truth which will require, after interpreting it, to ask what kind of work bears witness to those neglected dimensions of language.

> Upon meeting others, a savage man will initially be frightened. Because of his fear he sees the others as bigger and stronger than himself. He calls them *giants*. After many experiences, he recognizes that these so-called giants are neither bigger nor stronger than he. Their stature does not approach the idea he had initially attached to the word giant. So he invents another name common to them and to him, such as the name *man*, for example and leaves *giant* to the fictitious object that had impressed him during his illusion. That is how the figurative is born before the literal word, when our gaze is held in passionate fascination; and how it is that the first idea it conveys to us is not that of the truth. (*OL*, 13)

Rousseau's fable presents the origin of language in an encounter with another human being. The very setting downplays from the start the representational or descriptive function of language. But the communicative function of language is also absent, for communication would assume another that can understand and respond. Language originates in the encounter with another *as other*. Rousseau characterizes the encounter as frightening, thus leading to flight, avoidance, and defense. By means of the myth Rousseau indicates the presence in language of a drive to cover this original strangeness. Indeed, it will be language itself that will become the cover that hides from man its own alarming origin.

One of the striking aspects of Rousseau's fable is the assertion that figurative language preceded literal language: "As man's first motives for speaking were of the passions, his first expressions were tropes. Figurative language was the first to be born. Proper meaning was discovered last. One calls things by their true name only when one sees them in their true form" (*OL*, 12). If the paradigmatic understanding of a true utterance would be the attribution to a thing of a property that it has in fact, then a figure would be a way of speaking of a thing through something that does not belong to it, factually speaking. A figure returns us to its object by way of something else. Such a detour is necessary—is not just plainly false—when there is no way to speak straight to the point, directly of the thing itself. It is because the encounter at the origin of language is with a human being as essentially other that the utterance will be figurative or hyperbolic.

The first word bursts out like a cry. It is the continuation of a movement of passion, of fear. It is a passionate utterance. There is an essential relation between the figurative nature of that utterance and the excess of passion. For passion is intrinsically excessive. Passion must be distinguished from need. Need can be satisfied, whereas passion is always disproportionate.[3] The passionate core of language is something hidden or covered in the use of language, but does not disappear from language.

To point out that the cry is a continuation of the movement of passion serves to distinguish it from a representation of an inner state. In the passionate utterance, language is not an instrument that serves to represent well-determined inner mental states; it is, as it were, a medium which allows for the continuation of a movement and its externalization. It is worth emphasizing this point, since it might so readily be assumed that language as we know it is at one's disposal, the tool one *requires* to say what one *wants*, therefore also in danger of being used as a screen, to hide behind as well as to project an image and show oneself in whatever light one chooses.

The first word uttered is not, in any language, the word "giant." That is an exclamation, a cry, raising the question of how such a cry can express an estimation of size. There is no external standard to measure size on that occasion, nor is there a mediate comparison to previous experiences of smaller objects. Moreover, the other is just another human being. So there is no factual reason for this sense of the enormity of the other. Since there is no external measure, man in the state of nature takes himself as a measure, his own feeling of existence. Rousseau suggests, through that myth, that man in the state of nature cannot but feel frail in relation to the appearance of the other. For there is an intrinsic disproportion between this fleeting sense of existence and the external appearance, the figure of another.

Yet Rousseau does not just say that such an encounter causes flight, but also that the gaze is held in passionate *fascination*. This capture of the gaze can be thought of as a mirroring relation.[4] The appearance of the other allows the identification that constitutes the primary and original notion or representation of the self. For to say that man in the state of nature has a sense of his own existence does not mean that he has such a representation. The first self-representation results from the identification with the appearance of another. The self-image is thus essentially deceptive, essentially alienated. In the Second Discourse Rousseau describes the split between man's sense of existence and his self-representation in terms of his distinction between "amour de soi" and "amour-propre."

The latter, vain love of oneself, is precisely dependent on representing oneself through a comparison with others. At the source of such a comparison is the identification that constitutes the very first notion of an ego. Alienation in self-representation allows the comparison and generates the general concept "man." For now I is equal to the other, identified as it is with the other's appearance.

In literal language, the language of concepts, or the language which describes what there is equally well, the self is already constituted in alienation, by way of a problematic identification. Hence deriving the origin of language from the passionate utterance is not just a theoretical question; it involves a central evaluative dimension. To recover the dimension of the passionate utterance in language is to uncover language that is not used as a screen and a defense, as a shield from the other and from one's own sense of existence. It means overcoming the alienation of the self in representation, which is at the source of all the reactive mechanisms of *amour-propre*. Returning things to their true size is not taking them literally, but rather providing a measure in language that addresses the excess at the origin.

5

The Dimensions of a Place

The Fifth Walk is probably the purest, most perfect of all walks. Practically nothing happens in it. The content of the reverie is so much its form that this walk might well constitute a limit case. Approaching the limit raises the question of the origin of reverie as a form of thinking, and whether, at the end, it is thinkable in terms of form at all.

Certain simple matters come together in this walk. As Rousseau gives up the riches of society for a willing poverty, life is reduced to its essentials and acquires a simplicity that borders on utter monotony. Existence is narrowed to its fundamental dimensions. But those dimensions in all their simple concreteness sound strangely poetic. Each resonates as a powerful figure underlying the literalness of human endeavors. First and foremost is the figure of the island. It is not an island in the middle of the ocean, away from everything, but one in the middle of a lake, thus surrounded by water in turn encircled by land, a place of solitude in the midst of the inhabited regions of the world. Rousseau is thrust on the shores of this island by his stormy relation to his contemporaries, a new Robinson, next to the mainland, refusing to be rescued.[1]

There are two islands on the lake: "In the middle of this beautiful, nearly circular expanse of water lie two small islands, one of them inhabited, cultivated and some half a league in circumference, the other one smaller, uninhabited, untilled, and bound one day to be eaten away by the constant removal of earth from it to make good the damage inflicted by waves and storms upon its neighbor. Thus it is that the substance of the poor always goes to enrich the wealthy" (81–82).

The removal of soil from the small island makes the larger one into a viable human environment, prior to cultivation and building. The earth of the uninhabited place is transferred to the use of habitation—or rather, that transfer is necessary to make habitation possible. The bounded island thus not only provides a figure for the limits of one's world, the surrounding circle of existence, but is also a place to establish oneself anew, a place that can become a dwelling.

Significantly, Rousseau intervenes to reverse the direction of transfer, from the rich to the poor, from the human to the animal. Rousseau's expeditions to the uninhabited island are an occasion to experiment with the formation of an animal colony, to populate the uninhabited island with rabbits especially brought from Neuchâtel.

It is tempting to think of the contrast between the rabbits' environment for breeding and the human place of dwelling in terms of what animals do in their environment as opposed to what humans do in their world. This would make man into a richer determination of the species of animals: a speaking animal, a political animal. Yet in the Fifth Walk Rousseau is mostly doing nothing: "Precious *far niente* was my first and greatest pleasure and I set out to taste it in all its sweetness, and everything I did during my stay there was in fact no more than the delectable and necessary pastime of a man who has dedicated himself to idleness" (83).

That very human capacity for doing nothing reveals the human being's difference from the animal to be that of having a world at all.[2] The very fact of having a world goes beyond any determinants of activity and passivity through which one thought to distinguish the human from the animal. Rousseau's stay on the island might seem to show his detachment from the world in all its richness and variety, but in fact that reduction and concentration in one place makes the dimensions of his world more manifest than ever.

Rousseau accounts for what there is, spans and measures his domain, by composing a botanical manual of the island's flora: "I did not want to leave even one blade of grass or atom of vegetation without a full and detailed description. In accordance with this noble plan, every morning after breakfast, which we all took together, I would set out with a magnifying glass in my hand and my *Systema Naturae* under my arm to study one particular section of the island, which I have divided for this purpose into small squares, intending to visit them all one after another in every season" (84). The preparatory system of coordinates, the exhaustive laying out of space, dividing the island into small squares for the purpose of inquiry, allows for detailed research in a specific area. But such "geometrical" spatiality contrasts with a different sense of space that pervades the Fifth Walk. For the very possibility of an exhaustive search assumes the prior delimitation of a space for search and must be oriented by that prior opening. If dividing the island into small squares makes it possible to enumerate what there is, then the desire for such accounting itself depends on a sense of the domain of existence which is opened *for* accounting. One might even say that it is *because* Rousseau is on an island or can experience his world as a limited whole that he is tempted at all to divide it and inquire into every part in detail.

Being at home in a place depends not just on being acquainted with things, facts, or events occurring in it, but also on acknowledging the limits constitutive of that place. Such limits are not boundary lines that delimit a *part* of space, but rather they open the possibility of taking something into account at all. Rousseau links his happiness on the island to this awareness of limitation: "it is very agreeable and wonderfully well situated for the happiness of those who like to live within narrow bounds . . . I cannot believe that I am the only one to possess so natural a taste, though I have never encountered it in anyone else" (81). This taste for "narrow confines" is further emphasized, somewhat paradoxically, by Rousseau's reference to the island as an "isolated place in which I had imprisoned myself" (83), and he adds, "I could have desired that this place of refuge be made my lifelong prison, that I be shut up here for the rest of my days, deprived of any chance or hope of escaping and forbidden all communication with the mainland" (82).

Rousseau spends his time at the limits of his world, on the shores of the island, as well as on a boat, drifting in the expanse between the inner and the outer shores of the lake, between the surface of the water and the face of the sky. At the limit, things recede while surfaces become manifest. Throughout the walk Rousseau makes a point of remaining on the surface and avoid stirring any depths, whether of the place or the soul that answers to it. Rousseau's botanizing first shows his concern with what is on the surface, with the plants covering the surface of the island. But surfaces are not just the background against which things stand out perspicuously. Surfaces also allow reflection, making the I manifest to itself by way of the world. Outer and inner surfaces meet and often echo one another: "From time to time some brief and insubstantial reflection arose concerning the instability of the things of the world, whose image I saw in the surface of the water" (87). Reflection, or thought, is aroused by the movement on the water. It is a return to the self by way of a movement on that surface rather than a figure reflected in it, thus allowing self-forgetfulness rather than a vain self-preoccupation. Balancing inner against outer, Rousseau further mirrors that description by another, later on, that describes the tranquility in which "pleasant and insubstantial ideas barely touch the surface of the soul, so to speak, and do not stir its depths" (90).

Surfaces are open expanses that allow the experience of space itself *as* an opening. Space as an opening is not just the lack of obstruction, mere emptiness, but what allows the happenings in it. It is the passing and fleeting disturbances that make space manifest as the opening of possibilities. So Rousseau contrasts the emptiness of complete silence which "induces melancholy" and "is an image of death" (90) with the silence experienced on the island, "a silence which is unbroken but for the cry of eagles, the occasional song of birds and the roar of streams cascading down from the mountains" (81). The cry breaks the silence but thereby makes it manifest. Such silence is not the mere lack of noise but the possibility of what can be heard. Just as the surface of the water is revealed by the momentary ripples that disturb it, so is the soul revealed in its potentiality by the "pleasant and insubstantial ideas" that barely touch its surface (90). Thus the unchanging and timeless space of what is possible is not the opposite of the ephemeral and the passing, but rather is brought out by it.

Surfaces also meet and delimit each other—the water from the earth and land and water from the sky. Added to the original figure of limit as the surrounding circumference, we find limitation internal to the constitution of the place, articulating it, as though limits were dimensions of a space. Where dimensions can meet, they delimit each other. The balance of those dimensions is the point of rest. Rousseau is at the meeting point that holds together and separates sky and water, as in the original separation of the waters above and the waters below through which a world is created out of chaos.

To further elaborate this other sense of space, limits, and the repose they offer, one must reflect on the transformation of walking, the fundamental figure for thinking in the *Reveries*, which in the Fifth Walk becomes a kind of aimless drifting on the water. Beyond inquiry and its exhaustive divisions, and beyond thinking figured as walking, are the surroundings that allow these activities. Resting in one's surroundings is figured by Rousseau's description of passively being supported by the monotonous *va-et-viens* of the waves: "I would row out into the middle of the lake when it was calm; and there stretching out full-length in the boat and turning my eyes skyward, I let myself float and drift wherever the water took me, often for several hours on end" (85). The shift from walking to drifting reveals a state of mind that is even deeper than the reverie, or a dimension of the reverie which would not normally be associated with that state. There is certainly a sense of release in reverie, but there is also a stress on the activity of the imagination, the process of wandering from one thought or image to another, in a free play of the soul. If reverie is a way of wandering, then the Fifth Walk reveals that free play to be dependent on the very opening of an expanse for movement. The release reveals the open expanse and the way in which *it* supports everything.

This idea of release onto the supporting element shifts the emphasis fundamentally, from the individual and his modes of being in the world to the world that allows those ways. Repose now depends on abandonment, letting oneself be supported by the world, floating on the waters of the lake. The Fifth Walk brings not only a deepening of the understanding of the dimensions of being in space and time, but also a shift of perspective, a turn. Whereas what was mainly at stake in understanding the movement of reverie was the temporality constitutive of the subject of experience, in the Fifth Walk the time of the subject seems to answer to the world itself, measured by the repetitive monotony of the diurnal, echoed and figured in the movement of the waves.

Rousseau's stay on the island takes its rhythm from the repetition of the everyday. The occupations of the day are divided into the botanical investigations of the early morning, the manual labor of late morning, the meditative wanderings of the afternoon, and the self-forgetful reveries of the evening, until night arrives unaware. He was "often reminded by the declining sun that it was time to return home" (85). The diurnal rhythm signals an affirmation of repetition, equally avoiding activity and passivity, as if shifting from what takes place in time to the intense presence of that place itself.

Repetition is also manifest in the movement of the mind, taking over the playfulness in reverie. A rhythm of repetition comes into play in the waves of the lake. The sheer pleasure of existence awakened through such repetition, beyond the rich exuberance of images of the reverie, is the formal limit, or the limit of the form of the movement of the imagination:

> As evening approached, I came down from the heights of the island, and I liked then to go and sit on the shingle in some secluded spot by the edge of the lake; there the noise of the waves and the movement of the water, taking hold of my senses and driving all other agitation from my soul, would plunge it into a delicious reverie in which night often stole upon me unawares. The ebb and flow of the water, its continuous yet undulating noise, kept lapping against my ears and my eyes, taking the place of all the inward movements which my reverie had calmed within me, and it was enough to make me pleasurably aware of my existence, without troubling myself with thought. From time to time some brief and insubstantial reflection arose concerning the instability of the things in the world, whose image I saw in the surface of the water, but soon these fragile impressions gave way before the unchanging and ceaseless movement which lulled me and without any active effort on my part occupied me so completely that even when time and the habitual signal called me home I could hardly bring myself to go. (87)

Just as he felt at the moment of awakening after the accident, Rousseau is beside himself, feeling his existence in the ebb and flow of the water that takes the place of the inward agitation of the soul. But in contrast to that momentary experience of awakening, Rousseau describes here a state in which the precious feeling of existence can be experienced lastingly. It is as though repetition mediated between the momentary shock of the accident, which allows the most intense sentiment of existence, and the play of the mind in which that sentiment is dispersed in the movement carrying along the contents of the reverie. Feeling existence in repetition allows Rousseau, despite his limited stay on the island, to conceive of eternal existence on it: "I was barely allowed to spend two months on this island, but I could have spent two years, two centuries and all eternity there without a moment's boredom" (82–83). Eternity is not captured in the idea of time going on forever. Rather, as in the awakening after the accident, it is an intense sense of the present:

> But if there is a state where the soul can find a resting-place secure enough to establish itself and concentrate its entire being there, with no need to remember the past or reach into the future, where time is nothing to it, where the present runs on indefinitely but this duration goes unnoticed, with no sign of the passing time, and no other feeling of deprivation or enjoyment, pleasure or pain, desire or fear than the simple feeling of existence, as feeling that fills our soul entirely, as long as this state lasts, we can call ourselves happy, not with a poor, incomplete and relative happiness such as we find in the pleasures of life, but with a sufficient, complete and perfect happiness which leaves no emptiness to be filled in the soul. (88)

The eternal present, the Now of existence, which provides a resting place for the soul, should be distinguished from the ever-passing present, pressed as it is between past and future. The latter is primarily understood in terms of the actual presence of sensations to the mind, while the former refers to the complete showing of the conditions of one's state. Whereas action and inaction assume the consciousness of a lack, the concern with something to strive for or to avoid, doing nothing intensely is the awareness of the co-presence of all possibilities and leaves no emptiness to be filled by the soul.

Existence is felt in concentrating one's entire being in a place. Concentration allows the mind to balance the various dimensions of that world, giving to each its proper weight and place, so that none takes over and obstructs the others. (Separation is, no doubt, one of the best ways of evading oneself.) The concentric island allows concentrated repose. This accounts for the multiplicity of fundamental terms found in the Fifth Walk: the island, earth, sky, water, the plant and the animal, time and space, self and other, the eternal and the passing. Their meeting point provides a measure, their coexistence creates a design or schema of one's world. Neither reality nor fiction, this spanning of the dimensions of the world can be called original figuration, as though at the limit state Rousseau experiences on the island, in which he "could not draw a line between fiction and reality" (90), when the reverie is empty of images, the surroundings themselves were opened by the creative imagination.

As he writes the *Reveries,* years after his stay on the island of St. Pierre, Rousseau contrasts the reveries on the island with the reveries in remembering that state. The former were "abstract and monotonous," the latter contain many more "charming" images, providing therefore "greater pleasure." At the source of the reverie, as it is revealed in its pure potentiality, there is repetition. Repetition would signify that the sense of the place cannot be held to.[3] It cannot be sustained in memory, having no substantial content; it is a meeting point, an intense presence rather than something present to the mind. It can nevertheless reappear through the movement of memory by the displacements or figurations of meaning. The playful movement of the imagistic reveries becomes a retroactive opening of the meaningful surroundings of existence. It is in recollection that the reverie is true to the original creative figuration that opens a world.

6

Giving Way to Inclination

The *Reveries* contains a striking number of stories of gift-giving, through which Rousseau elaborates an understanding of human give-and-take and also of meaning given in experience. The two dimensions are dependent, at least insofar as the release from the problematic relation to others can provide a different opening to meaning. The *Reveries* further allegorizes its own offering. But what it takes to eventually receive Rousseau's writing might be to realize that he does not give it *to* the reader. This is something of a given in the *Reveries*, creating a circle it might be impossible to evade without stealing one's way out of it.

At the beginning of the Sixth Walk, Rousseau recounts how he realized the significance of a detour he got used to making in his walks. This detour resulted from the wish to avoid encountering a crippled boy to whom he gave money each time he passed his way. The initial pleasure in giving turned into an irritating obligation that imperceptibly brought about the habit of the detour: "From that time on I felt less inclined to go that way; and in the end I unthinkingly adopted the habit of making a detour when I approached this obstacle" (94).

This banal story triggers a reflection on the nature of freedom and the bondage of habit. Set against the fundamental activity of the *Reveries*, the detour is a denial of the freedom of the walk. That determinate direction is forced upon Rousseau without his conscious notice; it restricts freedom of movement and obstructs the possibilities of experience. Rousseau points out that "this route was of no significance in itself." But the discovery of the reason for the detour "recalled successively a vast number of similar cases which proved conclusively to me that the real and basic motives of most of my actions are not as clear to me as I had long supposed" (94). Thus the detour is made to stand for "our automatic reactions." When Rousseau traces the inconspicuous common habit to the singular encounter, he assumes significance at the heart of the habitual: "There are very few of our automatic reactions whose cause we cannot discover in our hearts, if we are really capable of looking for it" (93). For the habitual is not conceptualized merely in terms of monotonous repetition, of mental inertia which impresses certain patterns of thinking and behavior in the mind. Characterized as a detour, the source of the everyday habit is traced to a significant avoidance, a missed immediacy.

Rousseau begins his reflection by noticing the mechanical habit. The automatism points to something left un-thought, which nevertheless determines one's way in the world. When the singular situation at the origin replaces the incomprehensible repetition—in grasping the meaning of the automatism—Rousseau's reaction is laughter. The banal and incomprehensible repetition gives way to the comic aspect of the contortions one goes through to avoid the encounter, an indication of life beyond the mechanical.

Returning to the source of habit does not mean going from the habitual to the fantastic or extraordinary, for what is revealed is itself ordinary. But it is important that the meaningful ordinary is recovered by and through attention to the habitual. There is no "other place" in which immediate authentic experience is procured, but only the everyday world from which one begins and to which one returns. Thus this story becomes one more allegory of autobiographical writing that is stretched out between the banality of the everyday experience and the singularity and uniqueness that are recognized in the recall that opens up the meaning of that experience. The encounter and the avoidance it provokes raise a more general issue of being true to inclination, of giving way to inclination, something Rousseau no doubt hopes to achieve in the *Reveries*. Indeed, at first, the encounter is an occasion for freely giving to another, but that inclination in turn becomes an obligation, the rejection of which causes the detour. Inclinations, in their contrast to obligation, are often associated with egoism. But Rousseau's disinclination to give is not the regrettable effect of such self-love. On the contrary, what is difficult for him is that he can no longer give freely and do good: "I know and I feel that doing good is the truest happiness that the human heart can enjoy, but I have been denied this happiness for many years now" (194).

Rousseau faces the problems internal to the manifestations of pity in society. Whereas in the state of nature pity is shown intermittently, on singular occasions, without any bonds being created thereby between giver and receiver, in society acts of charity at first performed with "an overflowing heart" bring in their wake chains of continuing obligation. By that Rousseau means not so much the obligation the recipient incurs, but rather that of the giver: "as soon as any unfortunate individual had me in the grip of a favor received, there was no more to be said, and that first freely chosen act of charity was transformed into an indefinite right to anything else he might subsequently need" (95).

Is a more natural relationship possible, in which free giving does not degenerate into a burdensome and binding obligation? That is, can there be *commitment* without such double bind? Rousseau indeed envisions a contract to "form a kind of society" following *naturally* upon giving:

> I know that there is a kind of contract, indeed the most sacred of contracts, between the benefactor and the recipient; together they form a kind of society which is more closely knit than the society

which unites men in general, and if the recipient tacitly promises his gratitude, the benefactor likewise commits himself to continue showing the same kindness as long as the recipient remains worthy of it, and to repeat his acts of charity whenever he is asked and is capable of doing so. These are not explicit conditions, but they are the natural consequences of the relationship which has just come into being. (97)

This contract appears at first very different from the one Rousseau's name is usually associated with. Not only does it come into being in the wake of giving, but it seems to arise out of a fundamental asymmetry or inequality as one side shows kindness and the other gratitude. Yet the problem raised by this specific form of contract is not unrelated to the question of the emergence of man out of the state of nature to form a society. Can society arise out of nature while being true to nature, or is it constituted essentially against nature? Can there be a commitment that follows upon natural inclination, or must it be assumed that the degeneration of natural man, the forming of reciprocal dependencies, an equalization through reactivity, are necessary to lead man to the position in which he can enter a contract altogether? And is it necessary to assume that the ability to contract depends on the development of the problematic calculation of self-interest? This is a rather grim, though not farfetched, interpretation of Rousseau's *Second Discourse*. Ever since the first theories of the social contract, this notion has been considered in the light of the idea of striking a deal to satisfy mutual interests through social cooperation. Since the notion of a contractual relation is one which is taken from the sphere of economy, one assumes the contract essentially to depend on the sphere of economics, the give-and-take that underlies human relations.

Clarifying these matters might require going into the problems pity poses in the state of nature and in society. Without denying that the degeneration of love of self into self-love is a serious obstacle to the formation of a social contract, Rousseau's discussion brings out that it is no less important to realize what happens to pity, the other original natural inclination: "all of our natural impulses, including even charity itself, can change their nature when we import then into society and follow them unthinkingly and imprudently, and often become as harmful as they were previously useful" (95).

Already in discussing pity in the *Second Discourse* Rousseau broadens the scope of that notion so as to include under it many concepts that would not usually be associated with it: "In fact, what are generosity, mercy, and humanity, if not pity applied to the weak, to the guilty, or to the human species in general" (OI, 54). Importantly, Rousseau problematizes pity by linking it to language, as well as to reading and writing.

Even in the pure state of nature there are complexities of immediate identification. Rousseau establishes a paradoxical relation between the recognition of misery and pity when he insists on using the word "commiseration" for the natural sentiment of pity, while claiming that "misery" is a word that has no meaning in the state of nature. That play on words formulates a dilemma: if the recognition of a lack, for which commiseration is the appropriate response, depends on language unavailable in the state of nature, wouldn't the distance opened by language work in turn against the arousal of immediate pity? Pity would function through an indeterminacy principle: the more it is perfected, nuanced, the less is it possible to completely and immediately identify with the suffering.

The problem is even more acute when pity is directed to a collective ("the weak," "the guilty," or "the human race in general"). In order to generalize pity, one needs the general terms to refer to the collectivity pitied, but in Rousseau's *Discourse* it is precisely the development of such generalized concepts, allowing comparison, that signals the decline from nature, the development of reflection that cripples action. This inverse relation is brought to an extreme in Rousseau's figure of the philosopher reflecting on the problems of society in general. Philosophy is what isolates him and what moves him to say in secret, at the sight of a suffering man, "Perish if you will; I am safe and sound" (OI, 54).

This naturally leads to ask what happens to pity and identification in writing and reading. In the *Discourse* Rousseau considers an example from Mandeville, who describes the situation of "an imprisoned man who sees outside his cell a ferocious animal tearing a child from its mother's breast, mashing its frail limbs with its murderous teeth, and ripping with its claws the child's quivering entrails" (OI, 45). Rousseau's attention to the complete textual context makes this an example of the power of particularity in writing: Mandeville, whom Rousseau portrays as "the most excessive detractor of human virtues," is *forced* by his own description of a particular scene to depart from his cold and subtle style.

This observation recapitulates the problematic relation of general concepts and pity, but also adds that a complete shift can occur in writing and reading about those matters. Writing and reading have power but also danger. Rousseau hints at the latter when he writes that "one notes *with pleasure*" how Mandeville is forced to pity. A slight shift of perspective, or the introduction of another spectator, makes the emotion turn from horror and pity to smug pleasure. It is not surprising, then, that in the fullest elaboration of the problematic relation of expression and pity, involving the concepts of distance, particularity, writing, and *amour-propre,* Rousseau takes his reader to the theater:

> Every day one sees in our theaters someone affected and weeping at the ills of some unfortunate person, and who, were he in the tyrant's place, would intensify the torments of his enemy still more; like the bloodthirsty Sulla, so sensitive to ills he had not caused, or like Alexander of Pherea, who did not dare attend the performance of any tragedy, for fear of being seen weeping with Andromache and Priam, and yet who listened impassively to the cries of so many citizens who were killed every day on his orders. (OI, 54)

This juxtaposition of pity and theater is not, despite appearances, an endorsement of theater for its power to revive feelings long forgotten, but rather, it suggests that in society pity requires something like the position of a passive spectator or an outsider to the scene. Just as with Mandeville's prisoner, the situation described is one where no action can be taken—because of the very nature of theater, one might say, but equally because of what pity has become. Active participation would change the state of mind completely. Pity does not disappear in society. Instead, it allies itself with dubious moral attitudes; it is an identification that represents neither one's true capacity to act morally nor one's true motives. In society, pity and egocentrism are no longer opposed forces, as they were in the state of nature, but states of mind that subtly cooperate.[1]

Rousseau acts in society no longer. Expelled from all social commerce, his excommunication returns him, as he writes the *Reveries*, to a state of nature. "Unable to do good to myself or to anyone else, I abstain from acting; and this state, which is only blameless because I cannot avoid it, makes me find a sort of satisfaction in abandoning myself completely and without reproach to my natural inclination" (99). A peculiar freedom is revealed in abandonment, one very much at odds with the idea of freedom as autonomy associated with Rousseau's notion of the general will. It is now a freedom of giving way to inclination, realized by following the bent of one's nature: "I have never believed that man's freedom consists in doing what he wants, but rather in never doing what he does not want to do, and this is the freedom I have always sought after and often achieved, the freedom by virtue of which I have most scandalized my contemporaries" (104).

The dependence on others in society makes every motive into an ulterior motive, turns every action into a reaction. In such conditions freedom resides in what is unmotivated, giving up on willing itself and abandoning oneself to inclination. It remains to be seen whether this abandonment can, unexpectedly, provide the occasion for giving freely.

One of the fundamental difficulties in giving is that it generates an expectation to receive. That expectation is projected upon the giver, fixing his appearance in the eyes of the recipient. It is no longer possible to see the giver without any interest. A condition of giving freely would thus be the anonymity of the giver to the recipient, the lack of a known countenance of the giver. Many of Rousseau's narratives of giving are organized around gifts given to children, who do not yet recognize him as long as grownups do not instruct them. Moreover, one of the thoughts that Rousseau most enjoys entertaining in his walks is of being unknown. "If my face and features were as completely unknown to men as my character and natural disposition, I should be able to live among them without suffering, indeed I might take pleasure in their company as long as I was a complete stranger to them; abandoning myself freely to my natural inclinations, I should still love them if they paid no attention to me" (101).

This thought develops into an elaborate fantasy of total invisibility as Rousseau imagines what would happen to him if he had King Gyges' ring. Invisibility would allow him to act as the minister of Providence performing scores of merciful or equitable acts: "If I had been invisible and powerful like God, I should have been good and beneficent like him" (101). In the end Rousseau thinks it would be better after all to throw away the imagined magic ring, and with it the fantasy of invisibility. But what would it mean not to give up visibility altogether—for instance, keep on writing—yet also avoid having his appearance determined by others' expectations?

Rousseau returns to something like a state of nature. But the natural creature, in its solitude and singularity, can be repellent and frightening. The attempt to restore nature in the midst of artificial society creates what might look to all like a monster. The frightening aspect of man in the state of nature was an important issue of

Rousseau's fable of the origin of language. Language originates in this repellent encounter from which bursts the cry of fear that measures the disproportion between the appearance of the other and the self's sense of existence. In the story that opens the Sixth Walk, the encounter involves the problem of giving to a crippled boy who evokes pity and provokes avoidance. It is a situation that appears asymmetrical, unequal, and nonreciprocal, where one has to give, go out of himself toward the other who receives. The asymmetry of the situation is emphasized by the fact that Rousseau is giving to a child. Their difference of size makes one, as it were, a giant in the eyes of the other. Just as in the narrative from the *Reveries* on the habit of the detour that recoils from giving to the crippled boy, so, in the myth on the origins of languages, the recoil from the giant generates the detour, or turns into the habit in which develops the literal word, or the comparative concept of the genus "man."

A general concept is a detour in language that does not reach the thing immediately and in its singularity. The concept strays from the direct course to the thing, generates discourse. Often habit is appealed to in order to explain the formation of abstract terms out of the particularity of experience.[2] What Rousseau adds to this empiricist understanding is the idea that at the basis of habit there is avoidance of, or defense against, the immediate encounter—and the gift it keeps in reserve. Rousseau raises the question of how singularity can be given and received in all its uniqueness, beyond discursive detours, beyond the indifference of the concept or the correspondence of a tasteless truth, but above all in overcoming the avoidance from the other. What raises hope that this could happen is the fact that, in the original recoil, the situation is after all completely symmetrical, a situation of reciprocal avoidance.

Being so caught in the net of expectations can only contribute to Rousseau's paranoid self-consciousness in writing the *Reveries,* his sense of being accompanied everywhere by the fixated gaze of others. Rousseau must expose himself without making a show of himself for those spectators. In one way or another, this is a question that he has addressed in all of his autobiographical writings.

In the *Confessions* the fundamental episode that determines the mode of revelation of truth as a confession—the story of the ribbon—is, importantly, an episode of *theft*. It creates a chain of guilt, debt, retribution, and atonement. Writing is part of that chain, attempting to atone for a sin by giving truth to another. Thus to reconceive the conditions of giving and receiving is also to go beyond the confessional mode in autobiography.

In *Rousseau, Judge of Jean-Jacques,* Rousseau does more than confess. The text is constructed as a dialogue in which he prosecutes, defends, and judges himself. In this way Rousseau closes himself off from the judgment of his fellow men without avoiding judgment. It is therefore a work which assumes *proofs* of innocence. Despite or because of the closure of the condition of judgment, there is a serious problem for Rousseau in offering his work without opening up once more the threat of misjudgment. This is evident in the singular ways Rousseau plans to present his book to the world. Rousseau describes them in the epilogue, "Histoire du précedent ecrit." A young Englishman who visits him, a stranger to his immediate circle of acquaintances but in his eyes the minister of Providence, receives a copy. Rousseau then became worried that, despite his precautions, this Englishman was indeed in consort with those who harmed him. He decides to place his fate and the proof of his innocence in the hands of a complete stranger: he will write an address to the French nation, then copy and distribute it in the street to unknown passers-by of pleasing aspect, and thus get a chance of reaching a person of good faith who is not part of the plot against him. But the most peculiar attempt Rousseau describes is to deposit the manuscript on the altar of the cathedral of Notre-Dame. The victimization that Rousseau feels brings him to present the protocol of his trial as an offering to the One who makes the Last Judgment.

It is difficult to read Rousseau's account of the various schemes he devised for transmitting his writings, not just because of the anxiety that transpires through those pages, but also because they seem to show, beyond sensible doubt, that he had gone out of his mind. Such stories might be taken as proof that Rousseau was by then beyond recovery. Is it possible in that case to commit oneself to read the *Reveries* without having preliminary assurances about the sanity of its author? This would at least require the reader to check automatic defenses, and get over the various modes of avoidance in encountering such painful exposure.

In the *Reveries* Rousseau is no longer concerned about passing his work on to future generations, into the right hands:

> I wrote my first *Confessions* and my *Dialogue* in a continual anxiety about ways of keeping them out of the grasping hands of my persecutors and transmitting them if possible to future generations. The same anxiety no longer torments me as I write this. I know it would be useless, and the desire to be better known to men has died in my heart, leaving me profoundly indifferent to the fate both of my true writings and of the proofs of my innocence, all of which have perhaps already been destroyed for ever. (34)

Without proofs of innocence, there are no stagings of judgment. Instead, it is understood that innocence, as far as life as a whole is concerned, cannot be proved, or more precisely that it is not a matter of proof. It is part of the very concept of innocence that it must now appear in writing, beyond the stability of proof, argument, and judgment. If such innocence is another name for nature, then the exemplification of nature cannot take the form of a confession or a testimony to be judged.

Rousseau recognizes that he can no longer be assured of the fate of his writings: he must assume that every word he writes is liable to be distorted, every drop of meaning stolen from his work. Thus he would need not only to leave the writing to the mercy of God, but also *write* beyond human commerce. This other writing presents itself as writing beyond judgment, meaning both writing that attempts to consider further the immediacy of the proper name, rather than the discursivity of judgment, and writing that is incomparable.

The *Reveries* is written without the obligation of giving it to others. The ultimate victim is released from all obligating social relations. But that same victim, supposedly to be pitied, is the one who can give more than anyone can receive. Assuming that what Rousseau gives is his writing, the *Reveries*, then the problem is also how to receive it, read it beyond any expectation.

The *Reveries* constitutes free giving in being gratuitous writing, written for nothing and for no one. The author who gives retains his distance, remains a stranger to his readers. Rousseau's distance is not mysterious and tempting. It appears out of the succession of everyday and banal incidents that are collected in the *Reveries*. "I neither hide them nor display them" (34) he writes. Nothing is hidden, no secret given away, no sin to be confessed or judged. The uniqueness of the writing of the proper name, the singularity of autobiography, does not assume any riddles, not even those of the trade of writing. The open ordinariness of the *Reveries* is precisely what makes those stories owed to no one. Their graceful lack of mystery, their complete exposure, does not allow the reader to appropriate and thereby master them.

Exposure accepts the excess of meaning; abundance is revealed in abandonment. It is this abundance that can constitute a gift freely given, raising the question of what form reading should take, when meaning is laid out on the surface of the page, offered yet unintended. The first condition for receiving is letting Rousseau remain a stranger, not giving in to the temptation of intimacy. To let the terms that Rousseau put on the page do their work, to come to terms with the writing, would require accepting distance. Only thereby does the free gift of meaning become possible in abandonment. Only by giving up the wish to return Rousseau to life is it possible to experience the ways in which his writing is haunting.³

Giving freely must also allow another to receive without making that other a prisoner of gratitude, avoiding the chains that tie the giver to the recipient. It is giving without generating debt, guilt, or obligation. For that to happen, meaning should be such that in being given it does not seem to belong to the giver. This would also make it possible to speak through someone else's words, without thereby stealing meaning (another way of persecuting Rousseau). That lack of property rights over what is given can be elaborated by way of the idea of abandonment. Yet what is thus abandoned is still not what anyone could take as they wish. One has to be lucky enough to win that meaning, as it were by chance. When something falls into one's hands by chance, it is unintended and beyond expectation.

This relation between the given and the accidental is initially developed in Rousseau's Second Walk as he relates the story of his accident and awakening. This coincidence hints at a basic connection between being determined by the *accidental,* the contingent, and a heightened awareness of the present. In relation to the opening of the Sixth Walk, one could also say that the concept of chance belongs to the idea of the singular encounter insofar as avoiding it is the source of the habitual. This would turn the immediacy of experience into a field of opportunities, passing occasions for meaning, making the having of experience depend on taking the chance.

The role of chance in giving comes up when Rousseau tells of a walk during which he and his wife encountered a group of girls led by a nun. As they watched the children playing, a man selling wafers came by with his drum and wheel of fortune looking for customers. Rousseau paid him enough to let each girl draw a number on her turn. Yet as the author of the scene, Rousseau is not merely relying on good luck, and asks the operator of the wheel to cheat "and make as many lucky numbers come up as he could . . . Thanks to this stratagem nearly a hundred wafers were distributed, even though none of the girls drew more than one ticket" (144).

Rousseau binds the writing of the *Reveries,* accidentally or not, with chance. As he takes his walks, he writes his thoughts on playing cards. One might well ask what could be the future of such writing. How can someone's luck turn upon reading the cards? And is it Rousseau that will finally be encountered face to face by the reader? (In fact, a few years after his death, in year II of the revolutionary era, Rousseau's face did appear as the king of clubs on a deck of cards—an ironic illustration of, among other things, the difficulty of the immediate face-to-face encounter.)

Being at the mercy of luck creates an instability in reading, never being certain whether or not one is justified, always at the mercy of caprice, and also having to find a way to be grateful for the opening of this field of thought, providing these unexpected moments beyond proof.

7

Leaves of Memory

Seldom does Rousseau's *Reveries* attempt to capture a reverie in writing. Even so, the Seventh Walk stands out insofar as it describes temporarily giving up the writing of reveries in favor of the practice of botany. Here Rousseau forms a series of exchanges, moving back and forth between the collection of plants and the recollection of reveries through writing. This movement between reverie and botany, determined by inclination and gravity alike, relates the various themes of that walk.

When Rousseau first tells of his botanical trips, early in the Second Walk, the reader might not attach significance to the detail that the leaves of the plants he collects lie between the pages of the book he carries, for books can serve to dry flowers. The English translation—"these pages will be no more than a formless record of my reveries" (32)—might further hide that "pages" in French is *feuilles*, the same word for book pages and for the leaves of the plants interspersed in them. But it is harder to miss the relation between flowers and thinking, as Rousseau finds himself "at the close of an innocent and unhappy life, with a soul still full of intense feelings and a mind still adorned with a few flowers, even if they were already blighted by sadness and withered with care" (37).

In Rousseau's account of his stay on the island, in the Fifth Walk, grasses and flowers manifestly become a substitute for books and writing: "One of my greatest joys was above all to leave my books safely shut up and to have no escritoire.... Instead of these gloomy old papers and books, I filled my room with flowers and grasses, for I was then in the first flush of enthusiasm for botany" (83–84). He emphasizes this replacement of the book with the plant by adding: "I went about asking people if they had seen the horns of the self-heal just as La Fontaine asked if they had read Habakuk" (85).

Rousseau does not merely contrast the collecting of plants to recollection through writing. That one can replace the other means that they share something in common, that the movement driving the one is retained or incorporated in the other. So Rousseau keeps writing, but he writes of plants. Some ambiguous sentences in the Fifth Walk unfold a fantasy of language coupled with its subject matter; as if writing of nature were literally writing *on* nature: "I set out to compose a *Flora Petrinsularis* and to describe every single plant on the island in enough detail to keep me busy for the rest of my days. They say a German once wrote a book on a lemon-skin; I could have written one on every grass in the meadows, every moss in the woods, every lichen covering the rocks—and I did not want to leave even one blade of grass without a full and detailed description" (84, translation modified). Even if Rousseau does not really intend to miniaturize words, to write on grass as one writes on paper, this idea of covering nature with writing that corresponds to every atom of it articulates an intimacy of language and nature, figuring the word as a flower that grows and blooms out of nature, rather than an artificial or conventional addition to it.[1]

The nature of the replacement of the word by the plant becomes the central theme of the Seventh Walk, devoted almost solely to Rousseau's botanical occupation. The walk is framed by this exchange. At the beginning, the writing of the reveries is abandoned in favor of botany: "I have only just begun to write down all my long reveries and already I can feel that I shall soon have finished. Another pastime has taken over and now absorbs me so completely that I have not even time for dreaming" (105). And towards the end of that walk, the botanical collection returns Rousseau to reverie: "It is the chain of accessory ideas that makes me love botany. It brings together and recalls to my imagination all the images which most charm it: meadows, waters, woods, solitude and above all the peace and tranquility which one can find in these places—all of this it instantly conjures up before my memory" (120).

Rousseau can easily move from reverie to botany and back because the two activities have no determinate purpose. The reverie could be called a free play of the imagination, a purposive movement of the mind without purpose. But botany as well, according to Rousseau, must be without extrinsic purpose. The vegetal kingdom is dispersed on the surface of the earth to attract man to contemplation out of pleasure. Any subsumption of the botanical occupation under an external interest, such as, for instance, medical purposes, would distort and harm that pleasure.[2]

The enthusiasm for botany is a result of following inclinations. That indulgence is justified in providing an antidote to the troubled state of mind Rousseau feels in danger of sliding back into. It is a soothing activity, not involved in the serious business of life. To follow inclination not only does not conflict with reason, but is, in Rousseau's condition, something reason allows or even commands:

> I am not trying to defend my decision to follow this whim; it seems very reasonable to me, persuaded as I am that in my present situation to devote myself to the pastimes that appeal to me is not only very wise, but very virtuous in the bargain: it is a way of preventing any seeds of vengeance or hate from taking root in my heart, and in my position to be able to take pleasure in any pastime is a sure sign of a character totally free of all irascible passions.

Botany is no mere pastime that entrenches Rousseau's detachment from human society. It is truthful in manifesting inclination beyond particular interests and desires. Whereas desire assumes an antecedent motive, inclination requires one to follow it so as to discover where it leads. Following whim, though indefensible, is necessary to discover what such inclination reveals about the consistency of one's constitution. The idea of inclination is then fundamental in another respect, in being identified with the leaning which reveals what is natural (the bent of one's nature). "I have no other rule of conduct than always to follow freely my natural leanings . . . all my inclinations are innocent" (105).

The botanical occupation reveals a necessity beyond anything that reason can determine and justify: "[reason] does not tell me why this particular activity should attract me and what charm I can find in a fruitless study where I neither make any progress nor learn anything useful" (106). It does not demand justification but acceptance, not by way of a ground or a reason, but rather, so to speak, as the earth that allows growth.[3] To acknowledge this dimension is to allow the concreteness of the singular to be an endpoint, the resting point of thinking without ground. The impossibility of justifying oneself, of giving grounds, might suggest why being-on-earth is being-alone-on-earth. One must be open to that contingency and accept it upon oneself, that is, make it part of the meaning of one's existence. The partiality of one's constitution is not to be rejected, but must be recognized and affirmed in following inclinations: "It is a strange choice and I should like to know the explanation for it. I think that, properly understood, it might add something new to the self-knowledge which I have devoted my last hours of leisure to acquiring" (107).

Rousseau associates botany also with a return to childhood. It is "a study which takes an old dotard like me, feeble, ponderous, slow-witted and absent-minded as I am, back to schoolroom exercises and childhood lessons." Botany returns thinking from its elaborate and complex forms to its primitive first steps. It is not an occupation from which one could learn something useful and progress, but rather one that remains close to matters that must be impressed on the mind. "My ideas are hardly more than sensations now, and my understanding cannot transcend the objects which form my immediate surroundings" (112). Simple collecting stands before (or after) various forms of systematization, theoretization, hierarchization, and conceptualization that impose structures upon the material.[4] At the same time it reveals something that escapes the elegance of higher forms of reflection, as though the instruction of the child occupied the same place where late in life justifications come to an end.

The elementary character of botany also links it with the simple, the ordinary. The repeated wave of enthusiasm for botany overtakes Rousseau when his strength to wander is lacking and he has neither books nor a garden nor a botanical collection. "Until such time as I can collect all the plants of the seashore and the Alps, and the flowers of all the trees of the Indies, I am making a modest beginning with chickweed, chervil, borage and groundsel. I botanize learnedly at my bird-cage, and every new blade of grass that I spot makes me say to myself with satisfaction: 'There's one more plant anyhow'" (106).

This acknowledgment of the plain or everyday is opposed to the attraction of the exotic and the elaborate. It is expressed in the exclamation that accepts repetition: "There's one more plant anyhow." Justifications come to an end with what is simple. But simplicity is to be understood in relation to existence, rather than in opposition to complexity. It is not the discovery of a substance simple in itself but rather the acceptance that there simply is what there is.

Accepting what there is means also foregoing any further depths. The everyday is the open, what is on the surface, its difficulties not a matter of hidden secrets or unfathomable depths. Flowers bloom for everyone to see, bringing Rousseau to raptures and ecstasies in discovering their "innumerable little tricks of fertilization" (84). Remaining on the surface, Rousseau contrasts the occupation of the botanist with that of the mineralogist "who scours the entrails of the earth and descends into its depth" (113). The study of animals fares no better, for it requires "to tear them apart, remove their bones, dig into their palpitating entrails" (114).

Trees, bushes, and plants are profusely disseminated on the surface as though "the clothing and adornment of the earth" (108), multiple detailed ornaments of that open face. The detail brings one back to earth, to the awareness of the concrete. It clips the wings of the imagination, pulls it away from obsessive fantasies and brings about a renewed investment in experience.

> It was even to be feared that my imagination, alarmed by my misfortunes, might end by filling my reveries with them, and the continual consciousness of my suffering might gradually come to oppress my heart and crush me finally under their weight. In these circumstances an instinct that is natural to me averted my imagination and, fixing my attention on the objects surrounding me, made me look closely for the first time at the details of the great pageant of nature, which until then I had hardly ever contemplated otherwise than as a total undivided spectacle. (107–108)

The attraction of the detail counters the sublime ecstasy sensed in imagining the totality of nature. That sense of unity with nature is liable to be nothing but a mystification, ultimately revealed as utterly ridiculous. So Rousseau recounts that in one of his walks he reached a place so remote and isolated that he felt he was the first mortal to ever set foot on this part of the earth. His imagination filled with pride, as if he had discovered a new world, until he came out of a thicket of undergrowth and spotted, to his amazement, a stocking factory.

The detail attracts, that is, it initially calls attention to itself, not as something already recognizable, but as something to be looked at attentively. Announcing itself from afar, it is arresting and engaging: "My eyes strayed unceasingly from one thing to another and inevitably among so great a variety of objects there were some which attracted my attention and held it for longer" (108). There is thus a certain "materiality" to the detail, attested by its capacity to make an impression without being immediately comprehended, to attract without being recognized.

A detail is not a thing. But it is also no recognizable *part* of a thing. It is *essentially* partial, meaning it gives the impression that there is more to be viewed, to be attended with care. Thus it draws the observer to interact with it further. One can dwell upon details. A connection is thus formed between the attraction to the detail and the idea of inclination. The essentially partial generates an unmotivated motion that reveals inclination.

The detail, estimated aesthetically rather than objectively, is small. There are no huge details. But it is not minimal, since the minimal is essentially one thing, with no details. The smallness of the detail creates a certain concentration and intimacy. Besides attracting attention to itself, the smallness also causes thought to gather around the detail, isolate it from the rest of the world, or rather close the world around it. There seems at first to be an inverse relation between the detail and the surroundings. Whereas the detail requires focus, awareness of the surroundings would require a release, being attentive to nothing in particular. Yet to the extent that both states escape direct involvement with things and facts, to the extent that both the detail and the surroundings are inconspicuous, they might be related, one leading to the other.[5]

This relation of detail and surroundings is clear in the botanical collection that is supposed to bring about recollection. It relies on the rootedness of the plant, its power to evoke its native soil. Plants in the botanical collection are reminders of surroundings. They bring before Rousseau's eyes the landscape of his past journeyings.

All my botanical walks, the varied impressions made by the places where I have seen memorable things, the ideas they have aroused in me, all this has left me with impressions which are revived by the sight of the plants I have collected in those places. I shall never again see those beautiful landscapes, those forests, those lakes, those groves, those rocks or those mountains, the sight of which has always moved me, but now that I can no longer roam in those happy places, I have only to open my flower collection to be transported there. The *fragments of plant life* which I picked there are enough to bring back the whole magnificent spectacle. This collection is *like a diary of my expeditions,* which makes me set out again with renewed joy, or like an optical device which places them once again before my eyes. (120, my emphasis)

The botanical collection does not merely refer back to the material environment of growth of the plant, but rekindles reverie by returning the imagination to those sights, impressions, and tranquility that accompanied the botanical walks. Botany is identified with material fragments picked up and collected, and reverie is airy, atmospheric, revealing the surroundings of thought, but one belongs to or leads to the other.

Rousseau thinks of that collection of fragments as a diary of his expeditions, thus all but explicitly linking it with that formless record (*journal* in French) of his walks that is the *Reveries.* Plants are identified with the written word, which itself is meant to recall the reverie, that is, to allow the return of the self to itself. The word that Rousseau uses to characterize the collection of his reveries is *recueil.* In French this word is related to picking flowers—*cueillir*—and also to a kind of self-retreat in *recueillement.* Can the collection allow recollection?

Plants grow in their environment. Their surroundings support and provide the potential of growth, but therefore are inconspicuous when one is engaged with the plants themselves. Similarly, in relation to language and meaning, we might say that the common life-world supports the possibility of understanding and communication of meaning. It allows things to appear meaningful in and of themselves. But therefore it is precisely not something that is immediately given expression.

The collection of plants further points to the problematic fate of meaning: it can be detached from its original life. It is the materiality of the fragment which allows a remnant of meaning to subsist. In the botanical collection these withered and dried up remains of flowers, leaves, and grasses are only fragments of life. Just as it is doubtful that those dead plants would carry their world with them, to be revived at will, so recollection might not be an active principle, lively and full of meaning, in and of itself. The plant is a memento, an external and partial fragment that functions as a sign of the life which it must evoke. It is not quite arbitrary, but neither is it to be assumed that detached from its original surroundings of life, it still can have, telescoped within itself and miniaturized, those surroundings.

In that collection of leaves whose last lines were written shortly before Rousseau's death, there reigns a profound melancholy. "I shall never again see those beautiful landscapes, those forests, those lakes, those groves, those rocks or those mountains, the sight of which has always moved me." This melancholy must be distinguished from the nostalgic or sentimental sensibility which sometimes characterizes the Romantic image of Rousseau, when he is portrayed as driven by a need for a symbolic unity with nature. In this last autobiography Rousseau is not returned to himself. Loss is present everywhere and conditions the appearance and movement of meaning. In approaching those strewn materials of meaning it cannot be assumed that they will speak for themselves. To acknowledge the failure of the return and overcome muteness would demand finding a way to collect the materials, to pick up the pieces in what might be arbitrary and unjustified ways. This would not allow gathering Rousseau's intention, but rather, gathering might bring meaning to rest beyond intention.[6] The lively movement that follows inclination gives way to gravity in which the material fragments allow the recovery of nature precisely by way of the destruction of the unity of living meaning, returning to earth what came out of it. It might be that only when words are severed from their life source, collected in memory, that they can complete the movement of meaning and bring out the truth upon which they rested.[7]

8

Circles of Destiny

The opening sentence of the Eighth Walk sets down the terms destined to be transformed in reading: "Meditating on my state of mind in all the various circumstances of my life, I am extremely struck by the lack of proportion between the ups and downs of my fate and the general feeling of well-being or dejection they have aroused in me" (123). Such disproportion might characterize certain circumstances of Rousseau's life, but the transformation of a miserable fate into ecstatic joy is probably a more accurate way to characterize the state he finds himself in at the end, and sums up the logic that governs the *Reveries* as a whole. Not just disproportionate, at this extreme point Rousseau's condition becomes difficult to assess at all.

The transformation of dejection into well-being should be precisely characterized, for it is where many of Rousseau's critics find him most unbelievable. Thus Kierkegaard writes in a journal entry "that there are those muddle-heads like Rousseau, who use the strongest expressions in declaring that suffering is nothing, suffering—it is a pleasure—that is, theoretically, for in practice he was extremely thin-skinned."[1] And when Nietzsche writes "Men like Rousseau know how to employ their weakness, deficiencies, and vices as it were as manure for their talents,"[2] the comment might not merely provide a sarcastic description of the logic of the *Rev-*

eries, but also identify Rousseau's sensibility with the vengefulness of slave morality, whose central characteristic is to turn necessary weakness into virtue. This, presumably, is to be distinguished from true *amor fati* that makes fate a matter of affirmation.

Rousseau often portrays his condition as something "that lay in wait for [him]" (27). Its very irrevocability and finality would demand to introduce such a notion as fate into the picture. Yet one might wonder whether this self-understanding is itself part of the problem. Wouldn't calling certain contingent and isolated events "signs of fate" make them appear inevitable and all-encompassing? Shouldn't the very language of fate be avoided? Maybe the solution to Rousseau's ills lies in refraining from the imposition of false necessities on experience.

Rousseau's initial claim about the disproportion between the ups and downs of his fate and his well-being appears less paradoxical if we keep in mind that such well-being is identified with the memorable pleasure of existence. It is this pleasure, independent of the satisfaction of desire, that can be experienced in the most adverse of times. The figure Rousseau proposes in the Eighth Walk to further reflect on the nature of the pleasure of existence is that of concentration: "It seems to me that I enjoyed the pleasure of existence more completely and that I lived more fully when my emotions were so to speak concentrated around my heart by my destiny and could not go spreading themselves over all the things prized by men" (123).

The self exists in the midst of things to which it is attached. The soul is originally expansive, related to things in its surroundings. As Rousseau writes in the Seventh Walk, "I cannot concentrate my thoughts entirely within myself, because independently of my will my expansive soul seeks to extend its feeling and its existence to other beings" (112). That multitude of diverse attachments, a "thousand different tastes," Rousseau writes, "kept my heart constantly occupied, so that I could be said to have forgotten myself"

(123). Indeed, it is precisely the disparateness and plurality of those attachments that allows one to desire constantly and thereby evade oneself. When everything is in order the self is scattered, in a state of constant agitation. "Adversity," on the other hand, "forces us to draw in on ourselves" (124). The transformation brought about by adversity consists in concentration, in recognizing oneself as a *center* of attachment. Thus the self exists in distinct ways, which might be called expansive (or expendable) and concentrated.

The figure of the circle refers back to the Fifth Walk, reinforcing the picture of isolation in the midst of the world, concentration being what the island on the lake allowed. The center of the circle is the point of repose, achieved by balancing the diverse attachments: "Under pressure from all sides, I remain upright because I cling to nothing and lean only on myself" (126). This is not a withdrawal from the world onto a vanishing point of selfhood, but rather isolation by way of the recognition of the involvement of the self in its world. Instead of a multiplicity of desirable things, an inner unity or consistency emerges in concentration. To bring out the circle of which one is the center would be to make the things one is attached to into a world that belongs to the "I."

The sense of malevolent destiny arises when the multiple attachments created by the expansive soul in turn ensnare the self. It is possible to think of Rousseau's plight as his being caught in the web of ties which are now experienced as "secret plots" "in which I had long been unwittingly entangled" (125). The attachments turn into chains, since others are internal to the structure of desire (which is to say that self-love underlying desire is always reactive, whereas love of self is expressed in independence).

> When I see each of us, ceaselessly occupied with public opinion, so to speak extending his existence around himself, keeping almost nothing in his own heart, I believe I see a small insect forming out of its substance a large web through which alone he appears sensible,

whereas one would think it dead in its hole. The vanity of man is the spiderweb which he extends over everything that surrounds him; the one is as solid as the other; a single cobweb touched puts the insect in motion.³

In desire there is always an other against me, whose gaze I take into account. No heroic and authentic act of rebellion would be exempt from it: "When I used to protest so fiercely against public opinion, I was still its slave without realizing it" (126).

The problem is not just restricted to the sphere of desire, but rather concerns the experience of meaning in general. The movement of expansion and capture was central to Rousseau's myth of the origins of language, in which the first word attaching one man to another was essentially aggrandized and hyperbolic. The aggrandized image caught in mirroring reflection becomes the origin of the narcissistic dimension of selfhood. Bearing in mind Rousseau's elaboration of the excess at the origin of language and the movement of conceptual equalization, it is useful to return to a passage in the First Walk:

> Actual misfortunes *(maux)* have little effect on me; it is easy for me to accept those which I suffer in reality, but not those which I fear. My fevered imagination builds them up, works on them, magnifies them and inspects them from every angle. *(Mon imagination effarouchée les combine, les retourne, les étend et les augmente.)* They are far more of a torment to me imminent than present; the threat is far worse than the blow. As soon as they happen, they lose all the terrors lent to them by imagination and appear in their true size. I find them far less formidable than I had feared *(je les trouve alors beaucoup moindres que je ne me les étais figurés)*, and even in the midst of my suffering I feel a sort of relief. In this state, freed from all further fear and from the anxieties of hope, I shall learn from mere habit to accept ever more easily a situation which can grow no worse *(empirer)*; and as my awareness of it is dulled by time, they can find no further way of reviving it. So much good my

persecutors have done me by recklessly pouring out all the shafts of their hatred. They have deprived themselves of any power *(empire)* over me and henceforward I can laugh at them. (29)

The original French reveals a series of related ambiguities in this passage. Rousseau finds suffering in the experience of meaning, in the excess of meaning. Through the pun on *maux* (pains) and *mots* (words) he hints at the relation between language and victimization, as if human suffering were to be found at the origin of language. Rousseau further describes a movement of return from the hyperbolization of the imagination to what is of true size. The movement in which words are aggrandized is thought of as figuration, thereby making the return of things to their true size, their transformation, into a trans-figuration, going beyond the figure *(je les trouve alors beaucoup moindres que je ne me les étais figurés)*. But transfiguration is not literalization. Rather, literal language, governed by the common concept and by judgment, is precisely what ensnares the self, makes it dependent on others. The recoil from the hyperbolization of meaning to the common can only make things worse *(empirer)*. It allows others to hold sway *(empire)* over you.

To recognize necessity is to return words to their true size, leading them back from their expansion by way of concentration, without literalizing them. Literal meaning conceals that original excess. Desire, directed to this or that object, can provide the illusion that meaning is localized. But failing to confront the excess of meaning, even satisfied desire never achieves the required fit between self and world demanded for true repose. The revelation of the excess of meaning is the realization that meaning is implicit in all dealings with the world—a meaning which remains hidden but nevertheless determines one's actions. Being in such a space of unacknowledged meaning is being in a field of fate where transgression occurs unknowingly.[4]

Concentration that returns things to their true size permits crossing that field of fate. It overcomes the dependencies of desire by overcoming the plurality of objects of desire. Things come together in intense connectedness. Experience appears as meaningful to the extreme, and that meaning concerns the I, whose world then takes shape. But concentration also initially awakens the threatening sense of being surrounded by meaning. Instead of losing oneself in attachments, concentration returns to the I by way of the world. If initially, in the Second Walk, existence was felt suddenly, in all the surrounding things, then here what emerges is the menacing sense that all meaning has to do with the I.

In concentration, meaning takes the appearance of a sign. The sign stands as a warning that must be overcome in returning things to their true size. Excess of meaning gives the sense that everything encountered is an omen, contains some hidden significance, is a sign of fate. This is primarily an experience of persecution. Rousseau notices "some gesture or sinister look"; his experience contains, as it were, nothing but malevolent gazes. "Always too strongly affected by what I see or hear, and particularly by signs of pleasure or suffering, affection or dislike, I let myself be swayed by these outward impressions and can only avoid them by running away. A sign, a gesture, or a glance from a stranger is enough to disturb my pleasure or ease my suffering" (148). It is useless for Rousseau to try to habituate himself to those gazes, for the problem has to do with the excess of significance in experience itself: "A hundred times I have walked in public places and on the busiest thoroughfares with the sole object of learning to put up with these cruel looks; not only was I unable to do so, I did not even make any progress and all my painful and fruitless efforts left me just as vulnerable as before to being upset, hurt or exasperated" (132).

In the myth of the origin of language the first movement of signification is an essentially hyperbolized passionate utterance of fear. But such fear is tamed by the identification that is the source of the self and its reactive desires. It might be then conjectured that in returning things to their true size, escaping the dependence of desire, the threat of meaning will emerge once more. But this time it is encountered as the revelation of the menace of meaning externalized. The shift from the voice to the eye, from the song to the sign, changes the condition of language dramatically.⁵

The original model of the language of passionate utterance, while not exactly appealing to an expressive interiority, finds the source of significance in the outbursts of the soul as it expands towards what it encounters. In returning things to their true size, meaning is found in the object presented, externalized. In externalizing meaning, it becomes an essentially ambiguous sign, and, as such, also becomes menacing.

Rousseau emphasizes the intensity and effectiveness of signs: "What the ancients said in the liveliest way, they did not express in words but by means of signs. They did not say it, they showed it" (OL, 7). Signs are mostly visual, they are gestures or objects held before one's eyes. He further provides a series of examples that link the sign with the menacing:

> Darius, engaged with his army in Scythia, receives from the King of Scythia a frog, a bird, a mouse, and five arrows. The herald makes the presentation in silence and departs. That terrible harangue was understood; and Darius returned to his own country as quickly as he could. Substitute a letter for this sign: the more menacing it is, the less frightening will it be. It will be no more than a boast, which would draw merely a smile from Darius. (OL, 7)

The external sign is striking, impressive; it leaves a mark that bears no determinate meaning, and it is left to memory to give it meaning after the fact. "All that strikes me is the external manifestation [sign]. But afterwards it all comes back to me, I remember the place and the time, the tone of voice and look, the gesture and the situation; nothing escapes me. Then from what a man has done or said I can read his thoughts and I am rarely mistaken" (C, 114). The given leaves a mark which demands meaning. Its intensity allows its truth to resurface only in the repetition of memory and in the constructions of the imagination. It is in deadening the menace or fatality of meaning that the true necessity in the given is accepted.

In moving from a sense of fate to a recognition of necessity, the first step is to avoid personifying fate. If in the myth of the origin of language dependence was created in holding to the human figure of the other, in returning things to their true size one must overcome the original figure:

> When suffering people do not know whom to blame for their misfortunes, they attribute them to a destiny, and personify this destiny, lending it eyes and a mind that takes pleasure in tormenting them. In the same way a gambler who is angered by his losses will fly into a fury against some unknown enemy; he imagines a fate which deliberately persists in torturing him, and having found something to feed his anger on, he storms and rages against the enemy that he has himself created. (128)

The painful experience must be emptied of all intention before the face of destiny can turn into faceless and blind necessity: "In all the ills that befall us, we are more concerned by the intention than the result. A tile that falls off a roof may injure us more seriously, but it would not wound us so deeply as a stone thrown deliberately by a malevolent hand. The blow may miss but the intention always strikes home" (128).

Accepting destiny is moving beyond intention, treating the tile falling and the stone thrown alike: "The wise man sees in all his misfortunes no more than the blows of blind necessity and feels none of this senseless agitation" (128). Excessive persecution, which tore Rousseau away from all intentional attachments, allowed him to traverse the menace of meaning. Other people "ceased to be human"; Rousseau can no longer understand their behavior in meaningful terms:

Circles of Destiny · 93

[W]hen after vainly seeking a man I had finally to put out my lantern exclaiming: "There is not a single one left," then I began to see that I was alone in the world, and I understood that my contemporaries acted toward me like automata, entirely governed by external impulses, and that I could calculate their behavior according to the laws of motion. Any intention or passion that I might have supposed them to possess could never have provided an intelligible explanation of their conduct towards me. Thus it was that their inner feeling ceased to matter to me; I came to see them as no more than bodies endowed with different movements, but devoid of any moral relation to me. (127–28)

This description is peculiar, for it might be taken initially as portraying Rousseau's painful skepticism, his condition of being alone on earth, surrounded by mere automata instead of human beings. But just as in the First Walk solitude turned into the revelation of existence, so here Rousseau finds himself released precisely by this perception of others as machines.

Even more peculiar is that Rousseau's contemporaries are not the only ones who become devoid of all interiority in his eyes; Rousseau himself, released from all attachments, becomes a creature of the senses: "Governed by my senses whether I like it or not, I have never been able to resist the impressions they make on me, and as long as they are affected by some object my heart remains equally affected, but this passing emotion lasts no longer than the sensations that cause it" (132). Rousseau likens himself to an object tossed by the winds, with a complete fit between the impetus created by the impression of the senses and the corresponding moods or movement of the soul: "all my behavior is equally the work of a volatile temperament which is stirred up by violent winds but calms down as soon as the winds stop blowing; it is the ardour of my character that pacifies me. I give way to the impulse of the moment; every shock sets up a vigorous and short lived motion in me, but as soon as the shock is over the motion vanishes, and nothing that comes from outside can be prolonged within me" (134).

It is tempting to think of Rousseau as evading the moral sphere, even avoiding meaning altogether and giving himself up to the world as purely sensuous materiality. But the figure of concentration is another way of understanding the truth of the release from intention. Through concentration meaning achieves the stability and consistency of a thing, beyond interest or the endless deferral associated with desire.[6] Repose is achieved in drawing in, as though concentration left no more room for agitated motion, everything being at rest by holding together. Rather than a fit to the actual sensuous given, one might speak here of the actualization of meaning that leaves no hidden excess.

As with other issues, it is necessary to think through the considerations concerning fate and intention also in respect to the writing and reading of the *Reveries,* linking the deliverance from persecution with the destiny of the book. What would it mean to read the *Reveries* beyond intention? This is clearly an issue, since Rousseau himself thinks of his reveries as unintended. But it is not enough to *say* that he does not intend them to be read by anyone; it is necessary to show what it means to read them without assuming such intention on his part. A natural answer would be to say that readers just read into the work whatever *they* are concerned with. But this would not be reading beyond intention; it would be introducing the reader's intention into the writing. Meaning must exist beyond intention for writer and reader alike.

Insofar as it is possible to speak of a destiny of the *Reveries,* it is necessary for reading to take it upon itself to deaden all intention by fully actualizing meaning. This might be captured in a fantasy of work that releases, one by one, the various attachments or entanglements which plague the reading, past and present, of Rousseau's writings by tying everything together, bringing the agitation of meaning to rest by concentrating it intensely.

9

Exposing Theater

Entertainments and festivals figure prominently in the Ninth Walk, which addresses issues that were of great concern to Rousseau in his writings on the theater. Indeed, at this stage of reading the *Reveries* it becomes pressing to decide whether Rousseau is perhaps really staging a little piece in that text; whether his solitude is merely an act—whether, in sum, he is making a scene. For if interpretation reveals such a higher meaning in the seemingly ordinary surface of the text, then arguably the surface must have been crafted so as to represent that meaning. Adding to this thought the suspicion that Rousseau plays himself as uninterested, wholly self-absorbed, this structure of representation threatens to become something of a show.

Just as the "Letter to d'Alembert on Spectacles" originated in the encyclopedia entry d'Alembert wrote on Geneva, so in the Ninth Walk Rousseau takes personally a remark in d'Alembert's obituary of Madame Geoffrin. Rousseau takes D'Alembert's description of her relation to children as an indirect reference to him, reading between the lines the contrast between her good nature and his own monstrous behavior in abandoning his five children in an orphanage.

"Taking everything personally" might be a fair characterization of much of Rousseau's manner of thinking; it is his strength as well as what can be perceived as the weakness of a certain overzealous sensibility in his writings. The opening of the "Letter to d'Alembert on Spectacles," in which the question of the relation of the personal and the devotion to truth is broached, can serve as an example:

> I am at fault if I have on this occasion taken up my pen without necessity. It can be neither advantageous nor agreeable for me to attack M. d'Alembert. I respect his person; I admire his talents; I like his works; I am aware of the good things he has said of my country. Honored myself by his praises, I am in all decency obliged to every sort of consideration for him. But consideration outweighs duty only with those for whom all morality consists in appearances. Justice and truth are man's first duties; humanity and country his first affections. Every time that private considerations cause him to change this order, he is culpable. (L, 3)

At first these lines seem to express a rejection of the personal in favor of the universal duties of morality. But it is more accurate to say that theater becomes such a moral issue precisely because it was raised by someone Rousseau was associated with, and in relation to Geneva, his birthplace. There is no obligation for him to respond to d'Alembert, nor is it clear, on the face of it, what is so outrageous in d'Alembert's encyclopedia entry advocating the establishment of a theater in Geneva. Rousseau takes issue with it as it comes to touch his singular course of life.

The opening of the "Letter" resonates with the terms and language Rousseau will come to use in relation to the social contract. The distinction between the private will and the general will is here prefigured in a particularly interesting context, that of *writing*. Writing has its own force, its own authority, its own position in relation to the public and the private. Rousseau practically opens the *Social Contract* by pointing to that peculiar place of writing: "It will be asked if I am a prince or a legislator that I should be writing about politics. I answer that I am neither, and that is why I write about politics. Were I a prince or a legislator, I would not waste my time saying what ought to be done. I would do it or keep quiet" (*SC*, 141).

Writing belongs neither to the private nor to the public space, but initially can be characterized as the transition between the two. Whereas exercising the general will assumes in advance that an issue under consideration is of public concern, it is writing that makes something be of public importance. Such writing does not derive its authority from what is publicly justifiable. Rather, it relies on the self to speak for others. This means that dedicated writing does not require a person to overcome the singular circumstances of his life. It is by taking everything personally, without making it a private business, that makes it possible to reveal what is of general importance. Giving universal voice to one's concrete position in the world is what makes for exemplary writing.

Exemplification holds together particularity and universality. But it is not just the provision of an example of a given general law. Whereas things can provide examples of concepts or rules, only human subjects can act as exemplars, be representative. In exemplification something that is implicit, common yet unknown to all, is shown to be a possibility by the one who acts as a representative for others. It is thus necessary to draw a distinction between the agreed-upon state of affairs, and the possibility of another order to which expression is given by the exemplar. Whereas the example falls under an already given rule, in matters in which exemplification is essential the temporal priority is reversed, making the singular instance precede the law, thus allowing its realization.

Expression is essential to the idea of representativeness, for what is exemplified is not already there, given to all, but rather is realized in being expressed. Moreover, exemplification shows the very possibility of wording the world, producing new terms for existence in common. But if writing is to give expression *to* others, then the dangers of expression itself need to be considered further. How is representativeness to be distinguished from representation, which Rousseau decries in his *Social Contract?* How does expression avoid becoming a display, a show or spectacle for others? And can Rousseau's solipsistic communication in the *Reveries* still be conceived as exemplary for society?

In the Ninth Walk Rousseau recounts his involvement in the production of various scenes of which he then becomes the spectator. Apart from the lottery draw for the wafers, already discussed, two other scenes figure prominently as organized productions. The scenes were produced on the occasion of a celebration at La Chevrette "for the name day of the master of the house; his whole family had gathered to celebrate it, and to this end they brought out the whole brilliant array of noisy pleasures. Games, theatricals, banquets, fireworks, nothing was spared" (145). Significantly, both scenes raise the issue of the translation of staged amusement into the space of life.

> Gingerbread was being sold. A young man in the company had the idea of buying some and throwing the pieces one by one into the thick of the crowd, and everyone was so pleased to see all the yokels rushing, fighting and knocking one another down so as to get hold of a piece that they all wanted to join the fun. So pieces of gingerbread went flying in all directions and girls and boys rushed about, piling on top of one another and crippling themselves; everybody thought it a quite charming sight. Out of embarrassment I did the same as all the rest, although inwardly I did not find it as amusing as they did. (145–46)

Rousseau is the self-acknowledged author of the second scene, describing it as a "comic scene" for which he provides the *dénouement*:

Among other things I saw five or six urchins gathered round a little girl who still had a dozen or so pathetic little apples on her stall that she would have been only too happy to sell. The boys too would very much have liked to help her get rid of them, but they had only a few coppers between them, and this was not enough to make great inroads into the apples. The stall was a Garden of Hesperides for them, and the little girl the dragon that guarded it. The comic scene amused me for quite some time, but I finally provided a *dénouement* by buying the apples from the little girl and letting her share them out among the little boys. Then I had one of the sweetest sights which the human heart can enjoy, that of seeing joy and youthful innocence all around me, for the spectators too had a part in the emotion that met their eyes and I, who shared in this joy at so little cost to myself, had the added pleasure of feeling that I was the author of it. (146)

The first of the scenes serves to point at the ills of the theatricalization of social relations. The other is a production that is beautiful to the extent that it is also fair. Yet the difference between the two scenes is not merely that in the first one people pile up on top of each other and trample one another, whereas in the second one distributive justice is conducted in an orderly fashion, the apples shared justly. More importantly, the difference has to do with the nature of the involvement of the spectators. Whereas in the first scene the spectators gain a sense of aloofness and superiority along with the pleasure of mockery, in the second scene spectators and actors are present to each other and take pleasure in that mutual exposure.

The interest in the scene is deflected from the action and the various actors involved in it to its happy result, the joy of everyone concerned. Not just that of the children who give and receive the apples, but also to that of the other spectators to the scene, "for the spectators too had a part in the emotion that met their eyes." This shift from actor to spectator involves also Rousseau, the author of the scene. "For my part, when I have thought deeply about the sort of pleasure I enjoyed on such occasions, I have found that it consists less in the consciousness of doing good than in the joy of seeing happy faces . . . Indeed this is a disinterested pleasure which is independent of the part I play in it, for I have always been very attracted to the pleasure of seeing cheerful faces in popular rejoicings" (147).

This is not the pleasure of the spectator in an action, but the pleasure taken by a spectator in seeing the joy of other spectators, pleasure in expressions of pleasure. The twist in the form of theatrical enjoyment, in conjunction with the general concern of that walk with popular rejoicings, points back to the description of the public festivals in the "Letter to d'Alembert":

> [L]et us not adopt these exclusive entertainments which close up a small number of people in melancholy fashion in a gloomy cavern, which keep them fearful and immobile in silence and inaction, which give them only prisons, lances, soldiers, and afflicting images of servitude and inequality to see. No, happy people, these are not your festivals. It is in the open air, under the sky, that you ought to gather and give yourselves to the sweet sentiment of your happiness. . . . [L]et the sun illuminate your innocent entertainments; you will constitute one yourselves, the worthiest it can illuminate. (L, 125–26)

Turning Plato's cave into a theater hall, Rousseau makes the theatricalization of human relations comparable to the chains of the cave.[1] He clearly follows the structure of the myth of the cave in describing the overcoming of theatricalization by the festival in the open air, illuminated by the sun. Just as in Plato's myth exposure to the sun contrasts with the representations in the cave, so Rousseau's "Letter to d'Alembert" presents the idea of a theater beyond representation—the popular festival.

But what will be the objects of these entertainments? What will be shown in them? Nothing, if you please. With liberty, wherever abundance reigns, well-being also reigns. Plant a stake crowned with flowers in the middle of a square; gather the people together there, and you will have a festival. Do better yet; let the spectators become an entertainment to themselves; make them actors to themselves; do it so that each sees and loves himself in the others so that all will be better united. (126)

When nothing is represented, nothing staged, there is no self-contained fictional space standing in a problematic relation to the world; no more separation of actors giving themselves for the pleasure of others, from spectators identifying passively with fantasies that bar them from action. Spectators become an entertainment to themselves and enjoy their very gathering, their very visibility to one another, their exposure to each other.

In considering the problem of representation the aesthetic, the moral, and the ontological dimensions come together. Truthful-exposure (in particular in the writing of the *Reveries*) must be opposed to truth as adequation of representation and fact. The theatricalization of social relations is to be overcome by a theater beyond representation, And similarly, a society facing the decline brought about by political representation will be regenerated by a show of the general will.

An initial connection between theater and the general will can be drawn in considering that the general will must show itself. "All that can be said is that in general the more force a government has, the more frequently the sovereign ought to show itself" (SC, 196). This show of power or of sovereignty is threatened by representation. "Sovereignty cannot be represented for the same reason that it cannot be alienated. It consists essentially in the general will, and the will does not allow of being represented. It is either itself or something else; there is nothing in between" (SC, 198). The assembly of the people that shows the general will can be likened to the popular festival where all see each other, and only each other, so that no other representation takes place. And it is only in the co-presence of all those spectators to each other that a genuine act of will can take place. Yet this analogy seems to imply that the general will has no object other than the very being together, the co-presence or mutual exposure. In order to assess the validity of the analogy, it is necessary to go deeper into the relation between representation and decline as well as into the originary or regenerative nature of the general will that faces decline.

Every society, including well-formed societies, will suffer decline for reasons that are internal to the constitution of the social bond. Rousseau's experience of community is just as much that of its decline as of its formation: "The body politic, like the human body, begins to die from the very moment of its birth, and carries within itself the causes of its destruction" (SC, 194). This claim about the essential demise of the body politic should be contrasted with Rousseau's claim that the general will is indestructible. Sovereignty associated with the act of legislation of the general will must be sharply distinguished from the embodiment of contentful law in institutions that structure the form of life in the body politic.[2] The act of the general will is beyond representation in not relying on a standard external to itself. But its being an act of freedom means that there must also be a sense in which it is original or originating, rising from or against nature. The general will is indestructible because it is the manifestation of an unconditioned capacity, the absolute capacity to arise out of nature. To recover the origin is to originate society constantly against the background of inevitable decline. Constant creation, the life of the body politic, is the exercise of sovereignty or the exercise of the general will in the legislation of laws.

It is by virtue of being instituted—by virtue of the representation of its creative potential—that law faces decline. Political representatives are a symptom of the dialectical relation between origination and preservation with regard to the law. The preserving force of social institutions works not only in the service of the social order, but also against it. One could say that the very conditions of origination make mere preservation problematic. Preservation doesn't do justice to the original force in the formation of society. It is precisely because the original contract is an exclusion of nature that one might conceive of it as violent (despite its being unanimously agreed upon). As Rousseau puts it in the discussion of the legislator: "He who dares to undertake the establishment of a people should feel that he is, so to speak, in a position to change human nature" (SC, 163). In preservation the revolutionary power manifest in the formation of law is all but forgotten.

The idea of re-affirmation of the social bond as creation, as a return to the contract that originates out of nature, is the answer to ceaseless decline. Indeed, one need not assume a unanimous agreement in acts of the general will, as in the original contract. But such an act should testify to the original contract, contain within itself, in the absoluteness of its form, an acknowledgment of the original power, as if every time the contentful determinations of society are posited, a decision to reaffirm the existence of society is made manifest. In this sense the very gathering is essential to the content legislated by the general will, and its relation to the antitheatrical festival is no mere analogy.[3]

If acts of sovereignty generate community out of nature, and nature is the potentiality to regenerate society, then it also becomes necessary to set against society the standard of nature. Rousseau's position, which is different from exemplary representation of what society has in common, reveals nature excluded in the formation of society.[4] Not only at odds with society, excluded *from* it, but also excluded *by* it, by its constitution, Rousseau can be seen as standing for bare nature. The excluded is not the outlaw who is punishable by law, thus still within its bounds, but one who has no common language with society as a whole. Mythically, society arises out of nature; in time nature is recognized in what society excludes by its formation.

This last point clarifies also why Rousseau's exclusion does not make him a hero of tragedy. Tragedy has been traditionally understood as that "other" theater, intimately related to the regeneration of the political sphere. But Rousseau's abandonment is not only far from the tragic hero's encounter with fate; more importantly, to view Rousseau as a tragic hero would imply that he is still, in his solitude, attached to the fate of society. Indeed, we might imagine that his sacrifice is necessary for the very establishment of a future social form of life, that it will eventually work for society. Tragedy, from that perspective, is the source of new law or makes a new law possible.[5] But for Rousseau no such future is at stake. If there is an offering in the *Reveries*, it must be beyond return.

One might also point out that the circle of action of the tragic hero is characterized by a closure of meaning in time. That closure could be called the tragic hero's encounter with fate. It is in this sense that Walter Benjamin characterizes the logic of the tragic in relation to a completion of meaning. The tragic hero, as he puts it, dies of immortality.[6] The *Reveries* opens after everything is over, so to speak—after death—and its meaning develops by way of abandonment and exposure. To follow and reverse Benjamin's formula concerning tragedy, one could say that the *Reveries* is the afterlife of mere mortality.

Assuming the abandonment of meaning, the afterlife of the text has important consequences for the way in which the *Reveries* defies theater. One might think that the *Reveries*' shunning of all company is an attempt to recreate an antitheatrical state of absorption.[7] Indeed, one of the paradigmatic examples of an absorptive state is sleep. It is easy then to think of reverie or daydream as a similar state of being so completely absorbed in one's doing or lack of doing that this very absorption manifests an utter disregard for the gaze of any spectator or reader.

Yet it might be more accurate to say that Rousseau's antitheatrical stance starts from complete exposure. Complete visibility disregards the gaze of the spectator just as much as absorption. In order not to be mere display, this notion of exposure or visibility that is not *for* another must be characterized as a condition of meaning which is thus exposed, as foregoing the possibility of controlling meaning. That is, to control meaning is to retain language in the space of expectations of hopes, or in general of being for another. But this also means foregoing the idea of representation in language, for it is precisely the sense of language as representing that allows the idea of control over its effects. It is as though in representing language turned into a *means* for human purposes.

The pleasure in the text of the *Reveries* cannot be found through the presence to each other of author and reader. Instead their separation is brought to an extreme. Nevertheless something of the idea of the common exposure can be retained by realizing that the abandonment of meaning produces a gaze to which the reader is exposed. It is by acknowledging the abandonment of the text that the reader realizes he needs to be put on the line, that is, to be revealed by that book. Such reversal, the sense of being read by the *Reveries*, is what one would think of as a transferential effect of reading.

10

After Words

The *Reveries* is an unfinished work, the Tenth Walk barely broached when it ends suddenly. Rousseau's death, on July 2, 1778, disrupts the attempted literary rendering of life. The external fact of death arrests the inner unfolding of meaning, leaves the work unfinished, and thus seemingly precludes the full understanding of Rousseau's ultimate plan and intention in composing the *Reveries*. But it does not preclude bringing work to an end. Rousseau's text already challenged this separation of the internal and the external by foregoing the control of meaning. The end of that movement of meaning ought not to be identified with the completion of an action toward an intended goal. The end of meaning does not lie within the scope of the aims and purposes that characterize life. Rather, the end of life is meaning, and meaning is realized after life. Even if Rousseau had finished the book, this would not have relieved the reader from the task of bringing meaning to an end.

The death of the author should not be identified with the death of the work, but nor is it to be assumed that meaning lives on, speaking for itself. At issue is the fate of meaning and the position of a reader in relation to the afterlife of the text. Not only must the reader inherit or preserve the meaning, but also find ways of putting it to rest by tying everything together tightly, making it possible finally to take leave from the work.

What sense does it make to expend so much thought and effort in order to let go of work, to forego words? The aim of a devoted reading, it would seem, should be to follow Rousseau, to adopt his thinking or to have his language, so to speak, become one's mother tongue. It is particularly apt to ask such questions in reading the fragment of the Tenth Walk, all of which consists of one long paragraph about Madame de Warens, whom Rousseau called "Maman," "Mother."[1]

The Tenth Walk is melancholy, yet its opening is almost festive. "Today, Palm Sunday, it is exactly fifty years since first I met Madame de Warens" (153). A new tone is introduced in that walk, just before the end. It is pervaded by a certain grateful joy coexisting with the sadness of loss. Just as the Ninth Walk evolved out of occasions of celebration, so the Tenth Walk revolves around a day of commemoration, of remembrance: Rousseau marks the day, the exact day, by linking it to the religious commemoration as well to the particular fiftieth anniversary. He continues with a further counting of years: "She was twenty-eight then, having been born with the century. I was not yet seventeen."

This theme of marking a day as an occasion for commemoration is complicated: as Rousseau writes, "There is not a day when I do not remember with joy and loving emotion that one short time in life when I was myself." A distinction is drawn between the living memory and a marking of the day. For if memory is alive, why mark the day? How can one remember beyond keeping memory alive? Is it because meaning can die away that it is necessary to re-enliven it occasionally in memory? Or is it, on the contrary, the mark that allows the realization of meaning beyond the living memory?

The commemoration is an occasion for showing gratitude. Whatever remains of this Tenth Walk points to Rousseau's preoccupation with expressing such gratitude, paying back his debt. But at stake is no simple indebtedness. This act of thanking is an acknowledgment beyond any surveyable debt, for it is thanks for existence itself. Rousseau finds joy and loving emotion in the thought of "Maman" bringing him into the world. If she is not his natural mother, she nevertheless allows rebirth into a meaningful existence. This walk, at the end, returns to the beginning, to the idea of affirming one's own existence. And yet, this time, it is through his relation to another, to Madame de Warens, that Rousseau receives proof of his existence.

> There is not a day when I do not remember with joy and loving emotion that one short time in my life when I was myself, completely myself, unmixed and unimpeded, and when I can genuinely claim to have lived. I can say more or less the same thing as the Pretorian Prefect who was disgraced under Vespasian and went to end his days in the country: "I have spent seventy years on earth and I have lived for seven of them." Were it not for that short but precious period, I should perhaps have remained uncertain about my true nature. (154)

But that other through whom the self comes to itself is not present. Rousseau's recognition of the place of "Maman" in establishing his existence is belated; it is essentially the realization of truth in memory or out of loss. Rousseau's natural mother died in giving birth to him. He seems fated to experience the coming into existence as causing an irretrievable loss. A peculiar solitude which is at the same time an attachment is established at the heart of Rousseau's existence. His is a melancholic cogito.[2]

The Tenth Walk breaks off with the words "I resolved to employ my leisure hours in making myself able, if possible, one day to repay the best of women for all the help she had given me" (155). This sounds ominous, disappointment being often the fate of such noble resolutions. While this is the last line of the *Reveries*, it is possible to turn to an earlier account in the *Confessions* of an occasion in which Rousseau met again with Madame de Warens, shortly before the publication of his "Second Discourse," as he returned after many years to Geneva:

> Ah, that was the moment in which I should have paid my debt. I should have abandoned everything to follow her, to attach myself to her till her last hour, and share her fate, whatever it might be. I did nothing of the kind. Taken up with another attachment, I felt the tie which bound me to her loosening. For I had no hope of being able to turn my affection for her to any good purpose. I sighed over her but did not follow her. Of all the remorse I have suffered in my life this was the bitterest and the most enduring. By my conduct I earned all the terrible punishments which have never since ceased to fall on my head. I hope they may have atoned for my ingratitude. For there was ingratitude in my conduct, but my heart was too deeply wounded for it ever to have been the heart of an ungrateful man. (C, 365)

Cynicism would lead one to say that Rousseau's only resource is to be reunited ideally in memory, or to sentimentalize a relation to his eternal love in writing. Rousseau's account of his behavior towards Madame de Warens strengthens a suspicion that might already have arisen on various occasions in reading him: that he is incurably sentimental. A symptom of such sentimentality is precisely his indulgence in sweet memories as well as in self-reproach, while nevertheless avoiding action at the right moment. Such a condition is not unknown to Rousseau. He diagnosed it in discussing the function of tears in the theater. Moreover, whereas Rousseau idealizes his relationship with Madame de Warens, he seems to neglect his companion, Thérèse Le Vasseur. The lack of any similar show of affection toward the woman with whom he shared most of his life and who bore him five children—allegedly left in an orphanage at birth—brings Rousseau dangerously close to the figure of the tyrant in the theater.

It is tempting to identify as sentimentality the emotion present in many of Rousseau's writings. In the Tenth Walk Rousseau speaks of Mme. de Warens' kindness, tenderness, gentleness, and indulgence that formed his "naturally fervent heart" that was burning "with a new ardor." It would seem that her kindness educated his passion and sentimentality.

Sentimentality thrives on the fantasy of reuniting with a lost love object. In kindness there is a hint of sadness that comes of the acknowledgment of distance; it is often associated with the distance of memory, thus the presence of loss. Sentimentality is self-indulgent, but kindness essentially turns toward another.

Sentimentality is expansive, rash, and would close off all complications and throw away all irony. Kindness recognizes the frailty of the soul, the necessity to approach it carefully in awakening it, so as not to crush it in too strong an embrace. Kindness touches by way of careful and measured steps, its gestures are small and precise. Sentimentality opposes all crafting that would inevitably appear to it artificial, believing in extraordinary moments of utter authenticity. Kindness is associated with the domestic, it assumes that patient and indirect means are required to expose a surface for touching. Sentimentality depends on analogies provided by imaginary identification. Kindness works by way of hints of kinship, opening an unfigured space of relationships.

Although it is not necessary to opt either for cynicism or for sentimentality, how is it possible to draw a distinction between the ungrateful deed and the essentially innocent heart? Rousseau is not to be excused on grounds of weakness of the will. Nor is it so much the case that in order to fulfill his intention he made himself vulnerable to external adversities. Is it possible then to take Rousseau's word for it, or would it be necessary to take his words and find a way to redeem them? Caring for Rousseau's words is to risk adding another offense to his already problematic fate. For if identification is precluded, it is necessary to admit to a certain degree of arbitrariness in extrapolating the meaning of the *Reveries*. Imagining kindness makes it possible to take the chance.

Notes

Introduction

1. David Hume, *Essays, Moral, Political and Literary,* p. xxxi.
2. J. J. Rousseau, *Reveries of the Solitary Walker,* p. 27. Henceforth all references to Rousseau's *Reveries* will be provided immediately following the quote by page number. Reference to other of Rousseau's major works will include in addition to the page number the following abbreviations: *The Confessions*—C; *The Social Contract*—SC; *Discourse on the Origin of Inequality*—OI; *Emile*—E; "Essay on the Origin of Languages"—OL; "Letter to d'Alembert on Spectacles"—L.
3. The sense of a book as a totality often manifests itself in the movement of reading it. Stanley Cavell describes such a movement, which testifies to the connectedness of the book's world, in Thoreau's *Walden:* "The book's power of dialectic, of self-comment and self-placement, in the portion and in the whole of it, is as instilled as in Marx or Kierkegaard or Nietzsche, with an equally vertiginous spiraling of ideas, irony, wrath and revulsion. Once in it, there seems no end; as soon as you have a word to cling to, it fractions or expands into others" (S. Cavell, *Senses of Walden,* p. 12).

In order to conceive a book as a totality of meaning that is brought to expression by the movement of reading, we might need to treat the book *as* an idea that orients a movement of interpretation that is never fully adequate to it. Rousseau's *Reveries* further allows us to conceive of an ideal of the end, that is, a singular stable, unchanging concretization of the idea. A life realized in its meaning is such an ideal, a unique concentrated view of the world as a whole. It is in that sense that I speak of the ideal of the autobiographical book as a monad.

4. Although the concerns raised by the *Reveries* do not follow directly the work I have done on Wittgenstein's *Tractatus Logico Philosophicus* in my book *Signs of Sense*, some of them do echo issues of that book.

First, the *Reveries*, like the *Tractatus*, contains a paradox of reading. In the *Tractatus* the ultimate throwing away of the ladder revokes all that was previously written, thus creating the impossibility of meaningfully encompassing the book as a whole. The paradox of the *Reveries* is that the work is not for us—it is a book that Rousseau writes for himself alone. To read it unproblematically is to go against its fundamental premise. It is, therefore, a book that takes the question of the possibility of reading as internal to what it writes and problematizes to the extreme the conditions of meaningfulness. Like the *Tractatus,* too, the work requires a transformation in the position of the reader if it is to be read with understanding. It is a book that sets itself the task of bringing about such a transformation.

My reading of the *Reveries* brings to mind a further moment in my reading of the *Tractatus*—call it Wittgenstein's solitary moment—his claim that "The world is my world," which relates the experience of the world to my capacity to judge it for myself, to approach it as if I found it. Yet the *Tractatus* itself is not a work in which that truth of solipsism is exemplified, but rather a critique that opens the possibility of that relation to experience. Through Rousseau's *Reveries* I fantasize what it would be like for Wittgenstein to write the book for which he chose the title "The World as I Found It."

5. In *The Question of Jean-Jacques Rousseau,* Ernst Cassirer addresses the shifting form of Rousseau's writing and its relation to "Rousseau the man" by resorting to a dynamic figure:

> Anyone who penetrates deeply into this work and who reconstructs from it a view of Rousseau the man, the thinker, the artist, will feel immediately how little the abstract scheme of thought that is customarily given out as "Rousseau's teaching" is capable of grasping the inner abundance that is revealed to us. What is disclosed to us here is not fixed and definite doctrine. It is, rather, a movement of thought that ever renews itself, a movement of such strength and passion that it seems hardly possible in its presence to take refuge in

the quiet of "objective" historical contemplation. Again and again it forces itself upon us; again and again it carries us with it. (E. Cassirer, *The Question of Jean-Jacques Rousseau*, p. 35)

This figure of a movement serves Cassirer to distinguish the proper end of interpretation from the present fate of Rousseau's writings—the misappropriation of his thought. That unfortunate fate is characterized by Cassirer as the imposition of a fixed form upon a dynamic power. Instead Cassirer interprets Rousseau's thinking as containing an "inner strictly objective necessity" that "does not stand immediately before us in abstract generality and systematic isolation. It emerges gradually from the individual first cause of Rousseau's nature, and it must first, as it were, be liberated from this first cause; it must be conquered step by step" (p. 40).

Although Cassirer translates the idea of origin, the first cause of Rousseau's individual nature, into the various effects of an original potential, he does not consider the possibility that the full expression of nature requires also to follow up the movement of life beyond life itself. This emphasis on the end of the movement of meaning affects the method of intepretation. For Cassirer what is essential is a certain empathic identification (*verstehen*) with Rousseau the man and his times. But this method should at least take into account the problem of identification in Rousseau's writings and its culmination in the paradox of reading of the *Reveries*. Indeed, the *Reveries* constitutes a critique of identification, not just as a moral principle, but also as an interpretative principle. To preclude identification I emphasize that reading takes place as an afterlife of the text. I seek in the future of the *Reveries* (that is, in our present) the possibility of bringing its meaning to an end.

This aspect of my method of reading is inspired by Walter Benjamin. In particular I rely on his characterization of the idea of life and afterlife in the essay "The Task of the Translator":

> The idea of life and afterlife in works of art should be regarded with an entirely unmetaphorical objectivity. Even in times of narrowly prejudiced thought, there was an inkling that life was not limited to organic corporeality. . . The concept of life is given its due only if everything that has a history of its own, and is not merely the setting for history, is credited with life. . . . The relationship between life and purposiveness, seemingly obvious yet almost beyond the

grasp of the intellect, reveals itself only if the ultimate purpose toward which all the individual purposiveness of life tends is sought not in its own sphere but in a higher one. All purposeful manifestations of life, including their very purposiveness, in the final analysis have their end not in life but in the expression of its nature, in the representation of its significance. (pp. 254–55)

Benjamin indirectly relates the idea of the afterlife of meaning to Rousseau in the following passage: "The past has left images of itself in literary texts, images comparable to those which are imprinted by light on a photosensitive plate. The future alone possesses developers strong enough to reveal the image in all its details. Many pages of . . . Rousseau have a secret meaning which could not be deciphered by contemporary readers" (André Monglond, *Le Préromantisme Français*, quoted in W. Benjamin, *The Arcades Project*, p. 482).

1. "Here I Am Then"

1. In the Eighth Walk Rousseau writes: "after vainly seeking a man I finally had to put out my lantern exclaiming: 'There is not a single one left,' then I began to see that I was alone in the world, and I understood that my contemporaries acted towards me like automata" (127). In the Sixth Walk the figure is significantly different: "I feel for them," Rousseau writes, "as I would for characters in a play" (101).

    Other autobiographical texts raise doubts as to whether one is surrounded by human beings. Stanley Cavell speaks in similar terms of Thoreau's *Walden* and Nietzsche's *Ecce Homo*, referring to "their massive, insistent arrogance . . . an arrogance associated with some remarkable experiences . . . and associated with doubts that each exists among fellow human beings, doubts resolved ecstatically in something like new births, perhaps figured as the discovery of another world" (*A Pitch of Philosophy*, p. 39).

    Rousseau's skepticism is not the classical problem of the knowledge of other minds. That is, it is not primarily a problem of *knowledge*. One might say he knows his fellow men too well. It is not their souls that are veiled by their bodies but rather everything in them shows they have lost their souls. "They no longer exist since this is *their will*" (27, my emphasis).

Focusing doubt on the relation to others would seem to leave intact the dimension of one's relation to the world. And yet the two can be related in complex ways. Indeed, as will become clear, it is through the relation to another human being that Rousseau conceives of the very emergence of meaning, of the origin of language. This does not only mean that language is learned from others, but also that the other, the human other, is an archetypal figure in language.

2. Rousseau can provoke strong antipathy in sensitive readers. Voltaire, Schiller, Kierkegaard, and particularly Nietzsche seem to react not just to the contents of Rousseau's writings, but also to what they perceive as the relation between the man and his writings. Edmund Burke's reaction to the *Confessions* can stand for others as he writes that Rousseau recorded "a life not so much as chequered, or spotted here and there, with virtues, or even distinguished by a single good action. It is such a life he chooses to offer to the attention of mankind." (Quoted in C. Kelly, "Rousseau's *Confessions*" in P. Riley, ed., *The Cambridge Companion to Rousseau*, p. 302.)

Such reactions can be traced to the particular economy of the ordinary and the philosophical in Rousseau's writings. What might so infuriate readers is the constant reminder Rousseau provides of the ordinary in existence. His writings always originate in the anecdotal recounting of what happens to Jean-Jacques Rousseau but succeed in capturing an indefinable sense of anxiety and exultation that belongs to human existence as such. The animosity provoked by Rousseau's writing is therefore not external to the work of the text. It is to be expected that a thinker who makes *amour-propre* the source of evil would be keenly aware of the ways in which thought, even at its most sensitive, is threatened by a false heroism of the spirit.

The ordinariness exposed by Rousseau's writing can easily be mistaken for familiarity. Rousseau is the only philosophical figure who is often called by his first name alone, "Jean-Jacques." This has to do with his own way of referring to himself, for instance in the dialogue *Rousseau, Judge of Jean-Jacques,* but to point out this fact is merely to beg the question of the meaning of that familiarity. (Think how out of place a friendly overture toward Nietzsche would be: his writing always establishes distance and hierarchy.) The somewhat condescending wish to save Rousseau from his solitude is a false response, a mirror image of the animosity he can generate. Both are reactions to what seems so unthreatening and ordinary in his life. In other words, not only *amour-propre* but also pity has its dangers. Establishing an imaginary friendship with Rousseau provides yet another route of escape from the essential tension that his writing creates.

3. In particular, the question is to what extent the reverie can be true to the suffering at its origin instead of becoming a fantasized escape from reality. I. Babbitt writes: "It is not unusual for a man thus to console himself for his poverty in the real relations of life by accumulating a huge hoard of fairy gold. Where the Rousseauist goes beyond the ordinary dreamer is in his proneness to regard his retirement into some land of chimeras as a proof of his nobility and distinction" (*Rousseau and Romanticism*, p. 84). Kierkegaard, who knew all about renunciation and appreciated the stakes of autobiographical writing in philosophy, also wrote in his journals: "What Rousseau lacks is the ideal, the Christian ideal, to humble him and teach him how little he suffers compared with the saints, and to sustain his efforts by preventing him from falling into the reverie and sloth of the poet. Here is an example that shows us how hard it is for a man to die to the world". (Quoted in J. Starobinski, *J. J. Rousseau, Transparency and Obstruction*, p. 384.)

4. The closing moments of book I of David Hume's *Treatise of Human Nature* provide a significant contrast to Rousseau's condition. There Hume, despairing of the force of reason to lift itself out of its melancholy disposition, turns to everyday sociability to dispel the clouds of philosophy:

> Most fortunately it happens, that since reason is incapable of dispelling these clouds, nature herself suffices to that purpose, and cures me of this philosophical melancholy and delirium, either by relaxing this bent of mind, or by some avocation, and lively impression of my senses, which obliterate all these chimeras. I dine, I play a game of back-gammon, I converse, and am merry with my friends; and when after three or four hour's amusement, I would return to these speculations, they appear so cold, and strain'd and ridiculous, that I cannot find in my heart to enter into them any farther. (pp. 268–69)

No less interesting is another passage, a page or so later, in which Hume describes sliding back into philosophical speculations: "At the time, therefore, that I am tired with amusement and company and have indulg'd a *reverie* in my chamber, or in *a solitary walk* by a riverside, I feel my mind all collected within itself, and am naturally *inclin'd* to carry my view into all those subjects, about which I have met with so many disputes in the course of my reading and conversation."

Rousseau similarly would doubt the force of reason to overcome his tormenting doubt: "instead of wasting my efforts on pointless resistance, I wait for the moment when I can achieve victory by appealing to my reason, for it only speaks when it can make itself heard. Alas! What am I saying? My reason? It would be quite wrong of me to attribute this victory to reason, for it has little to do with it" (134).

For Hume the reverie and the solitary walk signal the return of philosophical melancholy. Solitude marks the advent of skepticism, and human society is one of the surest ways of recovering from it. Rousseau finds that society is what drives him to the most maddening condition; for him it is the reverie and the solitary walk that prove salutary.

5. I take Stanley Cavell's reading of Thoreau's *Walden* as a model for this aspect of my interpretation of the *Reveries*. He writes:

> It is hard to keep in mind that the hero of this book is its writer. I do not mean that it is about Henry David Thoreau, a writer, who lies buried in Concord, Massachusetts—though this is true enough. I mean that the "I" of the book declares himself to be a writer. This is hard to keep in mind because we seem to be shown this hero doing everything under the sun but, except very infrequently, writing. It takes a while to recognize that each of his actions is the act of a writer, that every word in which he identifies himself or describes his work and his world is the identification or description of what he understands his literary enterprise to require. (*Senses of Walden*, p. 5)

Cavell's understanding of writing and reading as opening a field of thoughtfulness becomes a central theme of his Moral Perfectionism. In his *Conditions Handsome and Unhandsome,* thinking once more of *Walden,* he describes the relation formed to the higher self in terms of the act of reading:

> As Thoreau sees the matter in the fifth chapter ("Solitude") of *Walden,* a grand world of laws is working itself next to ours, as if ours is flush with it. Then it may be a feature of any perfectionist work that it sets up this relation to its readers' world. What is next

to me, among other things, what I listen to, perhaps before me, for example, reading Thoreau's text, *Walden;* it is nearer than Walden may be, ever, and presents an attraction to its reader to find a Walden by not knowing in advance where it is and what it looks like. (p. 8)

The idea of the book, of writing taking up a force of its own, is powerfully expressed in Cavell's fantasy "that there is a place in the mind where the good books are in conversation, among themselves and with other sources of thought and of pleasure; what they often talk about in my hearing, is how they can be, or sound, so much better than the people who compose them, and why, in their goodness, they are not more powerful" (ibid., p. 4). It might be essential to Moral Perfectionism to embody the idea of the higher self in the medium provided by writing and reading. Presenting the idea differently, say by specifying certain contentful features, would risk turning the higher self into its own debased double.

2. From the Nature of Existence

1. Tracy Strong views the *Reveries* as raising the "possibility of the beautiful solitary soul as a solution—a critique of the world in which we live as well as of the beings who are of that world." He opposes this to fulfilling one's humanity in society, but also therefore thinks "that the cost of the society of the *Social Contract,* the cost of the life in which one is available in common to others, will be a loss of reverie and other delights" (*Jean-Jacques Rousseau, The Politics of the Ordinary,* p. 148). With this intuition Strong echoes Judith Shklar's claim that Rousseau presents excluding models of existence for men:

> What is strikingly novel is his insistence that one must choose between the two models, between man and the citizen. This necessity for choice, moreover, is not a call for a decision, but a criticism. It contains the core of Rousseau's diagnosis of mankind's psychic ills. All our self-created miseries stem from our mixed condition, our half natural and half social state . . . Nature is no longer an option open to men. . . . The alternatives are therefore not nature or society, but domestic or civic education. (*Men and Citizens,* p. 5)

But while the incompatibility between Rousseau's condition and life in society is obvious, the question is still whether one can conceive of the solitary walker both as excluded by *and* essential to society. Rousseau provides a standard necessary for society without exemplifying life in society.

The issue of the exemplification provided by the solitary arises for Rousseau before the writing of the *Reveries*. His break with Diderot was precipitated by reading in the latter's *Le Fils Naturel* that "only the evil man seeks solitude." The question is further provocatively raised in Diderot's letter to Rousseau of March 10, 1757, in which he writes "what an extraordinary citizen a hermit is" (quoted in E. Cassirer, *Rousseau, Kant, Goethe*, p. 8). But Rousseau seems at various junctures of his writing to embrace the paradox, even if it is not in the extreme form exemplified by the *Reveries*. In the letter to Malesherbes he writes: "Well may your men of letters shout that a solitary man is useless to all the world and fails to fulfill his obligation to society . . . It is something to set an example for men of the life they all ought to lead . . . If I had lived in Geneva, I would never have been able to publish the dedicatory letter of the *Discourse on Inequality*, nor would I have been able to speak against the establishment of the theatre in the tone I took." (Quoted in Starobinski, *J. J. Rousseau, Transparency and Obstruction*, p. 288.)

2. A too literal as well as a utopic reading of the myth of the state of nature would preclude treating its dimensions as something to be recognized in history, next to every human society. The quasi literal and the utopic readings equally neglect an important aspect of the myth of the species in the *Second Discourse*, namely the circle implicit in that work. Towards the conclusion of that discourse, Rousseau identifies the starting point and the end, the state of nature and the corrupt civil state:

> Here is the final stage of inequality, and the extreme point that closes the circle and touches the point from which we started. Here all private individuals become equals again, because they are nothing. Here everything is returned solely to the law of the strongest, and consequently to a new state of nature different from the one with which we began, in that the one was the state of nature in its purity and this last one is the fruit of an excess of corruption. (*OI*, 79)

This suggest the possibility of finding nature and with it the revolutionary task of reforming society in the dissolution of the social bond. What looks to all like a social state is in fact an aggregate of individuals that might understand the same language but have no meaning in common. The return to nature through the destruction of the social is indeed the starting point of the *Reveries*. Here too a certain circle can be recognized where the utmost victimization by society results in a solitude in which nature can become once more a standard for that society.

3. In thematizing the problem of solitude and its relation to writing, many interpreters are struck with the paradox of affirming total isolation. They point out that the relation to others is internal to the very idea of self-relation, making almost a logical point concerning the very possibility of descriptive language. Those reservations can be broadened into a more general difficulty of formulating a coherent solipsism. For language seems to be inherently social, making self-understanding dependent on the forms and categories provided in common existence.

Thus Judith Shklar comments on autobiographical self-knowledge: "No one but oneself can write one's life. To fully understand oneself, however, one must know more than that. One must know at least one other man in order to have some basis for comparison" (42). Shklar here paraphrases a passage from Rousseau's draft of the *Confessions:* "I want to make it possible that one may have at least one item of comparison, such that each person can know himself and another and that this other be me" (*Oeuvres Complètes*, p. 1149).

Significantly, Rousseau contrasts in the same passage knowing the other by way of oneself, a harmful form of comparison, and knowing oneself by way of another, which is how he provides for the self-knowledge of his readers. In the *Reveries* the position of total isolation must define a way in which complete otherness can lead to self-knowledge without thereby assuming any simple comparison. Thus I would think of Rousseau as providing a standard for measurement but not setting himself up as an object of comparison. The standard is part of the conditions for making judgments at all, whereas a comparison already is a judgment.

This idea of incomparability is captured by using the notion of singularity. The singular stands apart, isolated from society. Yet such isolation should not be understood along the lines of traditional metaphysical solipsism. Singularity singles out, thus isolates, but does not separate from the world. The "I" is alone-in-the-world, alone but precisely by revealing the world. That concentration of the world in a life is what makes it a standard.

Solipsism would be formulated through the possibility of refracting the world as a whole in one's own life. To put it in Wittgenstein's words, the truth of solipsism is that "the world is my world." In order to bring out the truth of solipsism it is thus further necessary to recognize a dimension of language which is not governed by the concept, the judgment and the comparison. Far from raising the threat of a private language, such solipsism is inherent in understanding the place of the subject in language.

4. This might explain a peculiar fact, noted by readers, that in the *Reveries of the Solitary Walker* it is very rare to encounter a reverie. Marcel Raymond writes: "The *Reveries of a Solitary Walker* contain few reveries in the proper sense of the word. They are not an intimate diary, a 'shapeless journal.' It is not so easy to break with centuries of rhetorical discourse." (Quoted in Starobinski, *Rousseau, Transparency and Obstruction,* p. 352.) And Starobinski adds: "Many pages of the *Reveries* are declarations of intention, lengthy preparations for the business of dreaming." Rousseau constantly sets up the stage as he describes the conditions of reverie rather than represent one. The remark in the opening paragraph, that he must first describe what led him to the state he is in, details accurately much of what goes on in the work.

5. It is enough to read Voltaire's letter to Florian of December 26, 1776, to realize what depths the animosity against Rousseau did in fact reach: "Jean-Jacques did very well to die. One says that it is not the case that a dog has killed him; that the wounds inflicted by his friend the dog have healed; but that on December 12, he decided to celebrate the *Escalade* in Paris with an old Genevan named Romilly; he ate like a devil and caught an indigestion; he died like a dog. It is so little a thing to be a philosopher" (J. J. Rousseau, *Oeuvres Complètes,* p. 1777, my translation).

No less interesting is the notice of Rousseau's death that appeared in the *Courrier d'Avignon* on December 20, 1776: "Mr. Jean-Jacques Rousseau died of the consequences of his fall. He lived poor, he died miserably; and the singularity of his destiny accompanied him all the way to the grave. We are sorry not to be able to speak of the talents of this eloquent writer; our readers must feel that his abuse of them imposes on us the most rigorous silence. There is every reason to believe that the public will not be deprived of his life and that one will find even the name of the dog that has killed him."

6. Hölderlin's poem "Rousseau" captures that ghostly existence: "Yearning you must haunt the shore, a shade, an outcast . . . And like the unburied dead you must roam about unquiet, seeking rest, and no one to the allotted way can direct you." Compare Rousseau's condition also with the opening of Nietzsche's *Ecce Homo:* "I live on my own credit; it is perhaps merely a prejudice that I am alive at all? . . . I need only to talk with any of the 'cultured people' who come to the Ober-Engadin in the summer to convince myself that I am *not* alive" (p. 33).

The image of being buried alive brings to mind the fate of Antigone who stands in that position of utter loneliness, between two deaths. Just as her position with respect to the law has been the basis for Hegel's reflection about the relation of tragedy to the political sphere, so in the case of Rousseau one should ask about the way in which his exclusion exemplifies something essential about the nature of law. See in this context my discussion of the Ninth Walk. I borrow the term "being between two deaths" from J. Lacan's discussion of the peculiar fascination exerted by the figure of Antigone in *The Ethics of Psychoanalysis*.

7. In *Of Grammatology* Jacques Derrida attributes to Rousseau an underlying metaphysics of presence and construes his writing as organized to recapture the lack of presence in speech. The following passage of the *Confessions* constitutes a paradigm for this interpretation: "I would love society like others, if I were not sure of showing myself not only at a disadvantage, but as completely different from what I am. The part that I have taken of *writing* and *hiding myself* is precisely the one that suits me. If I were present one would never know what I was worth" (C. 116). Derrida interprets that position of writing as follows: "In the *Confessions*, when Jean-Jacques tries to explain how he became a writer, he describes the passage to writing as the restoration, by a certain absence and by a sort of calculated effacement, of presence disappointed of itself in speech. To write is indeed the only way of keeping or recapturing speech since speech denies itself as it gives itself" (p. 142).

Derrida then quotes Starobinski, who describes "the profound law that commands the space within which Rousseau must move":

> How will he overcome the misunderstanding that prevents him from expressing himself according to his true value? How to escape the risks of improvised speech? To what other mode of communication can he turn? By what other means manifest himself? Jean Jacques chooses to be *absent* and to *write*. Paradoxically, he will hide himself to show himself better, and he will confide in written speech . . . Jean Jacques breaks with others, only to present himself to them in written speech. Protected by solitude, he will turn and return his sentences at leisure. (*Rousseau, Transparency and Obstruction*, p. 154)

Starobinski further extends to the *Reveries* the same model of writing he describes regarding the *Confessions:* "To suspend time and create a timeless reflection of one's life in writing, fixing happiness in a written image, is the expression of a wish to escape from the confusion and imperfection of the present; reverie never realizes this wish, yet it never ceases to strive in that direction" (p. 363).

Derrida himself does not relate to the *Reveries,* but the way he interprets the relation Rousseau forms between death and writing would make Rousseau's claim to be beyond life in that last book a further strategy of recovering presence:

> Such would be the writing lesson in Jean-Jacques' existence. The act of writing would be essentially—and here in an exemplary fashion—the greatest sacrifice aiming at the greatest symbolic reappropriation of presence. From this point of view, Rousseau knew that death is not the simple outside of life. Death by writing also inaugurates life. "I can certainly say that I never began to live, until I looked upon myself as a dead man" (*Confessions,* book 6). As soon as one determines it within the system of this economy, is not the sacrifice—the "literary suicide"—dissipated in the *appearance?* Is it anything but a symbolic reappropriation? Does it not renounce the *present* and the *proper* in order to master them better in their meaning, in the ideal form of truth, of the presence of the present and of the proximity or property of the proper? (*Of Grammatology*, pp. 143–44)

Even if one might grant that the movement of the writing of the *Confessions* is indeed as Derrida and Starobinski describe it, I have given reasons to doubt that Rousseau's writing of the *Reveries* should be thought of as governed by the same logic. The account of the aftermath of the accident in the *Reveries*, with its implication about letting writing lead its own afterlife, at least provides the beginning of an alternative picture. It is a task of the present book to further elaborate that alternative.

8. Michael Davis points to this dimension of writing in his elaboration of the issue in *The Autobiography of Philosophy*, constructing what might be called a dialectic of solitude and society. He begins by noting that solitude assumes society, indeed that Rousseau defines his solitude by contrast to society, thereby being still attached to society. Rousseau then seemingly provides a solution by forming a society within himself. He takes advantage of what Davis identifies as the split between the objective "I" and the subjective "me." The two are smoothly linked by the movement of the reverie. This proves to be an unstable solution, for the writing of the reveries introduces both a break and a potential public into that longed for continuity and completeness. But, according to Davis, it is precisely this break of writing that allows Rousseau to give up the illusory state of self-conversation and realize the necessity of adversity, of the external other, for happiness.

This interpretation consistently links together many issues in the *Reveries*. But it should be asked whether that book is to be read dialectically, i.e. ultimately overcoming Rousseau's utter abandonment and solitude. Further, it would seem that if there is a dialectical movement, it must not be limited to the one Rousseau is engaged in, but include the transformation of the relation of the text to its reader. How exactly does the text work for the reader? Is it merely the negative moment of the resistance of writing that breaks the illusory identification with Rousseau? Or can writing do its work, take a life of its own, allowing thereby to acknowledge both Rousseau's solitude and a meaningful relation to the reader?

3. Space, Time, Motion, and Rest

1. In connection with the idea of a nondirected movement of the mind, I want to invoke Kant's account of the aesthetic judgment upon beauty.

That purposive movement without purpose is said to reveal the faculty of representation as a whole, the subject in its potentiality for meaning. The aesthetic judgment, as Kant puts it, compares "the given representation in the Subject with the entire faculty of representations of which the mind is conscious in the feeling of its state"(*The Critique of Judgement,* ak. 204). Importantly, for Kant such a movement is not incompatible with rest or repose. As he puts it: "We dwell on the contemplation of the beautiful" (ak. 222).

The connection formed between Rousseau and Kant might not be justifiable directly, but it can be of significance in assessing Friedrich Schiller's criticism of Rousseau in his "On Naïve and Sentimental Poetry." Rousseau is, for Schiller, the sentimental type who "reveals no better tendency but either to seek nature or to vindicate her by art." He adds:

> His serious character never permits him, it is true, to sink to frivolity, but it does not permit him either to rise to poetic play. Sometimes gripped by passion, sometimes by abstraction, he rarely or never achieves the aesthetic freedom which the poet must maintain in relation to his material and communicate to his listener. Either it is his unhealthy excess of feeling which overpowers him and renders his emotion painful; or it is his excess of thought that lays shackles upon his imagination, and by the rigor of his concepts destroys the grace of depiction. Both characteristics, whose inner reciprocal workings and reconciliation in fact make for the poet, are present in this writer to an unusually high degree, and nothing is lacking except that they should manifest themselves in actual unison, that his intellectual ability should be combined with his feeling, and his sensitivity more combined with his thought. (p. 201)

Schiller's criticism, given the Kantian terminology that underlies it, concerns the relation between the understanding and the imagination in that movement which Kant calls the free play of the faculties in beauty. Instead of that harmonious free play, there is in Rousseau, according to Schiller, either too much understanding or too much imagination. If such harmony of the faculties is the condition of restful contemplation, of dwelling upon the beautiful, then Rousseau is portrayed as someone who ultimately craves only the agreeable, mere calm. This wish, according to Schiller, even affects his conception of the ideal:

Hence, in the ideal that he established for humanity, too much emphasis is laid upon man's limitations and too little upon his capacities; and in it one observes everywhere a need for physical calm rather than for moral harmony. His passionate sensitivity is to blame for preferring to restore man to the spiritless uniformity of his first state in order to be rid of the conflict within him, rather than to look for the termination of that conflict in the spiritual harmony of a completely fulfilled education; he would rather that art had never begun than that he should await its consummation; in a word, he would rather set his aim lower and degrade his ideal only in order to attain to it the more quickly and surely. (p. 202)

Rousseau might provide a more nuanced picture than Schiller is ready to grant him. For he takes into account not only the harmonious movement of the mind in reverie, but also failure and abandonment that are internal to the structure of written meaning itself. Rousseau thus relates the failure of beauty to the opening of a relation to another (his reader) that cannot be identified with the judgment of taste upon the work. Schiller's potentially infinite harmonious play of the mental faculties, which points to the idea without embodying it, might, in contrast, aestheticize the moral.

2. R. R. Descartes, *Meditations*, p. 12.
3. Such faithfulness is manifest first in the predilection for reverie, a self-absorbed mood which is akin to the solitary play of childhood. The very opening of the *Reveries*, "Here I am then alone on earth," could be read as an expression one could attribute to a child. (Stanley Cavell brings out how this sense of existing as a child among strangers, having to guess their language, is captured by the Augustinian vision of the entry of the child into language, which Wittgenstein chooses for the opening of his *Philosophical Investigations*).

Childhood and old age are often related in reactions to Rousseau, such as Mme de Stael's comment, speaking of "him, who should have been led like a child and attended like a sage." (Mme. de Stael, "Lettre sur les écrits et le caractère de J. J. Rousseau," cited in C. Blum, *Rousseau and the Republic of Virtue*.) Moreover, Rousseau is seen as always at risk of sliding into childishness, making a problematic rebuke of the whole world which the childish adult is willing to entertain in fantasy. Such childishness is also manifest in foregoing the sphere of work, of means. As J. Starobinski puts it: "Rousseau seeks to satisfy his desire without accepting the constraints imposed by the human condition. He wants to become a composer and musician all at once, without the bother of studying composition and music; this miracle is to be wrought by a grace immanent in the very intensity of desire"(*J. J. Rousseau, Transparency and Obstruction*, p. 60). This description recurs in many criticisms of Rousseau, presenting him as dreaming of an immediate, magical presence of the object of desire, disregarding any means required to achieve satisfaction. Maturity would be the acceptance of the necessity of work, of means to achieve ends. Yet work mostly has a definite object, aim, and direction to it. It is precisely this directedness, which does not allow it to be a model for thinking, that reveals or opens a world as a whole. It is a certain boredom, as Heidegger would think of it, *flânerie*, as Benjamin would call it, or idleness as Rousseau puts it—understood not just as a psychological state but ontologically—that stands a chance to reveal the world.

The notion of maturity should be further related to the idea of the revelation of nature discussed in relation to the Second Walk. For not only is maturity the most suitable time to engage in the arduous tasks of life; it comes to be associated with the stage in which a living being comes to manifest its potential most fully, thus to exhibit its essence. In Rousseau's account maturity is problematized by the belatedness of the child as well as by the melancholy of old age. This might require thinking of the fullest manifestation of essence, its fulfillment *in meaning* to be achieved only after life is over.

4. R. Descartes, *Meditations*, p. 12.
5. In the Dedication to the *Discourse on the Origin of Inequalities* Rousseau, addressing the republic of Geneva, similarly claims that there is no need for the city to advance or achieve anything more but rather to recognize and be content with the state it is in: "The more I reflect upon your political and civil situation, the less I am capable of imagining that the nature of human affairs could admit of a better one . . . your happiness is complete; it remains merely to enjoy it. And to become perfectly happy you are in need of nothing more than to know how to be satisfied with being so" (*OI*, 29). As the myth of origins recounted in the *Second Discourse* shows, that capacity to be at rest in one's present condition might be the most difficult thing to achieve.
6. Rousseau clearly refers to the chariot driver guiding his horses in Soc-

rates' myth of governing the soul, in Plato's *Republic*. He also refers to Socrates' understanding of philosophy as the art of learning how to die, in the *Phaedo*. This identification with the figure of Socrates is peculiar, for although Socrates is condemned by Athens, he insists on remaining part of it in dying. Moreover, he spends his last hours in the company of his disciples, engaged in conversation, rather than alone before death.

4. A Singular Truth

1. Rousseau writes in the "Letter to d'Alembert on Spectacles": "Never did personal views soil the desire to be useful to others which put the pen in my hand, and I have almost always written against my own interest. *Vitam impendere vero*: this is the motto I have chosen and of which I feel I am worthy" (L, 132).
2. In an important chapter of his book *Allegories of Reading*, entitled "Excuses," Paul de Man interprets Rousseau's account of the episode of the stolen ribbon in the *Confessions* as well as his return to it in the *Reveries*. De Man recognizes Rousseau's urge to confess through writing as an attempt to atone for the lie and its consequences. Yet at the same time that act is, according to de Man, Rousseau's attempt to excuse himself, to substitute writing for taking responsibility. The recurrence of the episode in the Fourth Walk of the *Reveries* shows the ambiguous nature of writing and its way of reproducing guilt instead of bringing peace. De Man further problematizes the revelation in a confessional mode by pointing to the *pleasure* in exposure that is implicit in the act of writing. If indeed there is a pleasure in exposure, then the confession is a further indulgence of the impulse that led Rousseau to lie.

    De Man further ties the retelling of the story to the form of writing of the *Reveries*. He argues that the presence of the writing effects of the lie cannot be located in a specific excuse pronounced in the Fourth Walk but, as it were, constitutes the entire text of that walk. Although Rousseau would present his writing in the *Reveries* as harmless gratuitous fiction, it is in fact an act of covering up, now disseminated over the whole text. It is writing itself that becomes the locus of the pleasure in exposure and excuse.

    De Man's interpretation raises a fundamental question about the notion of innocence and its relation to writing and meaning. Not everything is defensible about a human life, but the sense one gets in reading Rousseau is that life itself can be redeemed rather than excused. The issue, one must remember, is not whether Rousseau is guilty or not, but rather whether and how that lie can be consistent with a good character. Similarly, the question is whether writing can show good character (which is not to be confused with virtue). If character is manifest in life as a whole, then autobiographical writing could provide an image of life that would show innocence.

One way in which the supposed attempt to show innocence would turn into a mere excuse would be to make this exculpation an *aim* of the writing—as if the person writing desired that innocence, but the very involvement of desire in writing made its achievement problematic. Rousseau concludes the Second Walk with the words: "God is just; his will is that I should suffer, and he knows my innocence . . . everything will find its proper place in the end and sooner or later my turn will come" (45). This appeal to God might indicate that Rousseau does not take it upon himself to have everything find its proper place, that this is not his to bring about. The abandonment of meaning shows innocence not to be a goal, but rather an end. It is not up to the writer itself to bring meaning to an end. But what is required of the writing is the exposure that allows meaning to be abandoned. Such exposure should not be viewed, as de Man thinks of it, as an aim of desire.

To clarify this point consider that Rousseau's episode of the stolen ribbon narrates an original sin and can be read in relation to *the* original sin, that is, the story of the Fall: taking what is forbidden, accusing the woman, the emergence of desire, the awakening of shame, the lie and the concealment, as well as the expulsion of the pair. This parallel seems especially pertinent as Rousseau portrays himself in the *Reveries* once again alone in the world, in the state of nature like the first man. The association might indeed explain Rousseau's insistence on the origin of his sin in shame. If shame is the fundamental affect in the story of the garden of Eden, then innocence is not far behind.

Yet the myth of the garden of Eden distinguishes two senses of exposure and thus of concealment and shame. The first exposure reveals Adam and Eve to themselves and to each other as creatures of desire. Hiding their nakedness, they manifest shame in their nascent sexuality. Avoidance and shame are mutual and lead to concealment from the gaze of the human other. But there is also flight from a more fundamental exposure, the exposure of man to the divine gaze. In that instance nakedness would not be associated with desire, but would rather signify, as it sometimes does, utter vulnerability, fragility or finitude; call it the smallness of being so exposed on the face of the earth. Similarly, shame would not arise *from* someone else, but *in* oneself (for God is no finite other).

3. An elaboration of this important distinction would require us to discuss Rousseau's account of the origin of language in the *Discourse on the Origin of Inequality*. That account emphasizes the emergence of language out of the necessity of communication rather than the otherness that is intrinsic to passion. "Man's first language, the most universal, the most energetic and the only language he needed before it was necessary to persuade men assembled together, is the cry of nature. Since this cry was elicited only by a kind of instinct in pressing circumstances, to beg for help in great dangers, or for relief of violent ills, it was not used very much in the ordinary course of life, where moderate feelings prevail" (*OI*, 49).

4. I put the issue in terms of Lacan's famous constitution of the essentially narcissistic self in the mirror stage. I find many points of contact between Rousseau's analysis of the emergence of language in relation to love of self and Lacan's account.

5. The Dimensions of a Place

1. Recounting his stay on the island in the *Confessions,* Rousseau writes that he wants to "build, like another Robinson Crusoe, an imaginary dwelling on this little isle"(*C*, 594). In *Emile* we find the following enthusiastic appreciation of *Robinson Crusoe:*

> Since we absolutely must have books, there exists one which, to my taste, provides the most felicitous treatise on natural education. This book will be the first that my Emile will read. For a long time it will alone compose his whole library, and it will always hold a distinguished place there . . . What, then, is this marvelous book? Is it Aristotle? Is it Pliny? Is it Buffon? No. It is *Robinson Crusoe.*
>
> Robinson Crusoe on his island, alone, deprived of the assistance of his kind and the instruments of all the arts, providing neverthe-

less for his subsistence, for his preservation, and even procuring for himself a kind of well-being—this is an object interesting for every age and one which can be made agreeable to children in countless ways. This is how we realize the desert island which served me at first as a comparison. This state, I agree, is not that of social man; very likely it is not going to be that of Emile. But it is on the basis of this very state that he ought to appraise all the others. The surest means of raising oneself above prejudices and ordering one's judgements about the true relations of things is to put oneself in the place of an isolated man and to judge everything as this man himself ought to judge of it with respect to his own utility. (*E*, pp. 184–85).

That Rousseau likens his conditions on the island to that of Robinson Crusoe shows how nature can be found just next to society.

2. This transition from the human world to the animal environment, is, following Rousseau's analogy, a transition from the rich to the poor. But it is not the case that one world is rich and the other poor in contents or interest. Rather, it is possible to say, after Heidegger, that the animal is poor-in-world. (See Heidegger's discussion of the concept "world" in his *Fundamental Concepts of Metaphysics*.)

The association of Rousseau and Heidegger is in part warranted, as through the Fifth Walk the deepest intimacy is formed between Hölderlin's poetic thinking and Rousseau. In "Rousseau" Hölderlin echoes and responds to the pathos of the *Reveries*.

> How narrowly confined is our day-time here.
> You were and saw and wondered, and darkness falls;
> Now sleep, where infinitely far the
> Years of the peoples go drifting past you
>
> And some there are whose vision outflies their time;
> Abroad a god directs them, but, yearning, you
> Must haunt the shore, a shade, an outcast
> Cursed by your kin, and no longer love them,
>
> And those you name, whose coming is promised us,
> Where are those new ones, that by a friendly hand
> You may be warmed, where drawing near, that
> Audibly, you, lonely, speech, may sound then?

> The hall yields no response to your voice, poor man;
> And like the unburied dead you must roam about
> Unquiet, seeking rest, and no one
> To the allotted way can direct you.
>
> So be content! the tree outgrows
> His native soil, but soon will his branching arms
> The loving, youthful, then begin to
> Droop, and his head he will bow in sadness.
>
> Life's superfluity, the immensely rich
> That teems and glimmers round him, he'll never grasp.
> And yet it lives in him, and present,
> Warming, effective, his fruit contains it.
>
> You lived! And *your* crest too, though but once, yours too
> Is gladdened by the light of a distant sun,
> The radiance of a better age. The
> Heralds who looked for your heart have found it.
>
> You've heard and comprehended the strangers' tongue,
> Interpreted their soul! For the yearning man
> The hint sufficed, because in hints from
> Time immemorial the gods have spoken.
>
> And marvellous, as though from the very first
> The human mind had known all that grows and moves,
> Foreknown life's melody and rhythm,
>
> In seed grains he can measure the full-grown plant;
> And flies, bold spirit, flies as the eagles do
> Ahead of thunder-storms, preceding,
> Gods, his own gods, to announce their coming,

Heidegger does not refer to "Rousseau" but quotes a poem of Hölderlin's entitled "To the Germans" in the essay "The Age of the World Picture," which is an early version of "Rousseau.'" The exclusion of the direct reference to Rousseau cannot be accidental if we consider that in one of Hölderlin's most important hymns, "The Rhine," Rousseau's name occurs at a critical juncture:

> Of demigods now I think
> And I must know these dear ones

> Because so often their lives
> Move me and fill me with longing.
> But he whose soul, like yours,
> Rousseau, ever strong and patient,
> Became invincible,
> Endowed with steadfast purpose
> And a sweet gift of hearing,
> Of speaking, so that from holy profusion
> Like the wine-god foolishly, divinely
> And lawlessly he gives it away,
> The language of the purest, comprehensible to the good,
> But rightly strikes with blindness the irreverent,
> The profaning rabble, what shall I call that stranger?

Lake Bienne is named in the next stanza, forming a further intimate connection between Hölderlin's concern with water and Rousseau's repose on the lake in the Fifth Walk. And yet Heidegger dismisses that connection:

> Who is this stranger who remains other? In this stanza we find the name "Rousseau." We know that his name was inscribed only retroactively, in place of that of Heinse, Hölderlin's friend. Similarly, in stanza XI, verse 163, "by lake Bienne" was added later, in relation to the decision of naming Rousseau, for this is a place in which he sojourned. The original interpretation of the stanza must get rid of the reference to Rousseau. Even more: only by proceeding the other way around, that is, by starting from the sense of the stanza, can we understand the reason why the poet can also name Rousseau here. (M. Heidegger, *Hölderlin's Hymns 'Germania' and 'The Rhine,'* my translation)

This rejection of Rousseau's proper name in Heidegger's interpretation of Hölderlin's poetry becomes more striking once one draws a certain itinerary of the dissemination of Rousseau's thought, culminating in Derrida's *Of Grammatology*. It becomes clear that Rousseau is placed at the antipodes of the development of Heideggerian thematics, exemplifying the metaphysics of presence at its highest modern form.

Something else of importance takes place in Heidegger's choice to interpret the version of Hölderlin's poem entitled "To the Germans." It allows him to move from the fate of the proper name to that of the destiny of a nation. To trace the notion of poetic dwelling, which is elaborated for Heidegger through the reading of several of Hölderlin's river hymns (primarily "The Ister" and "The Rhine"), to Rousseau's Fifth Walk would problematize that move away from the proper name to the national spirit. The question raised for our reading is whether and how Rousseau's own solitary writing is to be thought of in relation to a common destiny. What are, in the broadest sense, its political dimensions, and does it require the dedication to the proper name? The Fifth Walk might indeed be the seemingly most distant point to any political concern, but that refusal of society might be related in unsuspected ways to the opening of a space for being together.

3. In accounting for the sentiment of existence it is important to avoid making it incompatible with a *meaningful* opening to the world. The simple reflexive sense of self might be the way Rousseau characterizes the sentiment of existence in the mythical account of the state of nature, but it is necessary to translate that description to reveal the corresponding possibility of a being that already exists within language and in society with others.

So as to avoid dissociating the world and the sense of self, Michael Davis characterizes the sentiment of existence as a second-order feeling: "in the Fifth Walk, happiness is not a matter of the content of one's feelings but rather consists in the feeling of feeling—the sentiment of one's existence" (*The Autobiography of Philosophy,* p. 189). As Davis puts it, "Reverie requires that one's senses be occupied but not so occupied that one's attention is completely given over to their objects. Only in this way does it become possible to feel oneself feeling and so experience the sentiment of one's own existence" (p. 179). This is why, according to Davis, the sentiment of existence arises in relation to perceptual experience that has practically no content, except for a certain rhythmic repetition.

> Rousseau has experience (he is alive) but of an almost indeterminate kind. At most his experience calls forth a weak impression of the transience of things temporal. Thus, insofar as reverie leads to thought, it leads to the sort of thought that applies equally to everything in the world. On the one hand, the experience that gives rise to reverie is sufficiently indeterminate to make it possible for us to experience our own experience; we have a sentiment of our own ex-

istence. On the other hand, because of this indeterminacy, our experience is not really of anything in particular and might have anything as its object . . . Accordingly what we experience in reverie is nothing in particular but rather being as such. (p. 180)

The problem with this account seems to be its minimalism. Davis assumes that only when one has so little content can one be aware of what underlies all meaning as such (as he puts it, the state in which "we sense ourselves in sensing the world and sense the world in sensing ourselves" [p. 180]). But it is hard to understand in what way this is an experience of *Being*, of what makes all things possible. Rather it is much more clearly an experience of the *fact* that one has sensations at all. If anything, even the movement of the imagistic reverie can provide a better model for the idea of sensing the potential for meaning than such a minimal self-awareness.

6. Giving Way to Inclination

1. The "Letter to d'Alembert" makes it clear that Rousseau is suspicious of any Aristotelian attempts to account for the effects of tragedy through a notion of catharsis. The problem to begin with is that one does not know which passions are purged and which strengthened: "Do we not know that all the passions are sisters and that to combat one by the other is only the way to make the heart more sensitive to them all? The only instrument which serves to purge them is reason, and I have already said that reason has no effect in the theatre" (L, 21).

    Rousseau adds: "In the final accounting, when a man has gone to admire fine actions in stories and to cry for imaginary miseries, what more can be asked of him? Is he not satisfied with himself? Does he not applaud his fine soul? Has he not acquitted himself of all that he owes to virtue by the homage which he has just rendered it? What more could one want of him? That he practice it himself? He has no role to play; he is no actor" (24–25). The catharsis in the theater is, more than anything else, the purging of conscience.
2. See for instance Hume, *Treatise of Human Nature*, book 1, 7, "On abstract terms."
3. Tracy Strong argues that Rousseau wishes for an immediate encounter with his reader, beyond representation, while his readers always insist

on taking him in a certain way, under certain presuppositions, from a certain perspective: "The panoply of interpretations are impositions of categories that seek to fix a person once and for all" (*J. J. Rousseau and the Politics of the Ordinary,* 29).

Immediacy beyond representation is achieved, according to Strong, in Rousseau's foregoing authorship, in an act of "de-authorization." What needs to be created through the writing, however, is the immediate relation between two human beings, so retaining the position of author would be one more way of re-creating the distance of representation and of raising oneself above the ordinariness that is common to all. Thus Strong writes that "the success of the project of the *Confessions* will be to annihilate the author of the book and replace him/it with a human" (18).

While there is no doubt that Rousseau mistrusts representation in writing and politics alike, we must ask how writing itself can allow thought beyond representation. In seeking immediacy, Strong downplays the work the text can do on its own. The immediate encounter from man to man is at risk of coming at the expense of the elaboration of a textual problematic and thereby turn into a wordless intimacy always risking mystification. The text becomes a means, a ladder one can do away with, to reach the immediate encounter. This is an even more serious issue in the *Reveries,* for assuming the possibility of immediacy in that text counters Rousseau's professed self-isolation. It is necessary precisely to assume the work of the text beyond the intention of its writer to allow for the fulfilment of its task in reading, in time. Thus indeed the author is overcome insofar as his intention is not authoritative, but the *medium* of writing remains as the field in which the higher meaning of the ordinary is revealed.

7. Leaves of Memory

1. This idea of placing a book in nature is figured in one of the anecdotes concerning the appearance of human industry in the midst of nature. Rousseau recalls "another botanical expedition, which . . . I had undertaken some time before on the Chasseron mountain, from whose summit one can see seven lakes. We were told that there was only one house on this mountain, and we should never have guessed the profession of its occupant if they had not added that he was a bookseller, and what is more, that he did a thriving trade in the region" (119).

2. Plants, as Rousseau understands them, are also associated with what does no harm. So in one of his botanical expeditions Rousseau tastes the berries of a bush, and after finding them tasty, eats about twenty of them to quench his thirst, watched in silence by his companion, a Monsieur Bovier, a resident of the area. One of Bovier's friends who arrived at the scene immediately exclaimed that the berries are poisonous. Bovier, like everyone in the area, knew that, but out of humility did not dare tell Rousseau. Rousseau came out of this incident slightly worried but with no harm to his health.

   The story relates plants and words that should have been uttered but were withheld. This further link in the exchanges between language and the plant suggests reading this incident in relation to Rousseau's discussion of the relation of truth and justice and the possibility of innocent fictions in the Fourth Walk.
3. In discussing Leibnitz's principle of ground Heidegger quotes from Angelus Silesius' *The Cherubic Wanderer:* "The rose is without a why: it blooms because it blooms, it pays no attention to itself, asks not whether it is seen" (M. Heidegger, *The Principle of Reason,* p. 41). Compare this to Rousseau's characterization of man in the state of nature: "each particular man views himself as the only spectator who observes him, as the only being in the universe that takes an interest in him, as the only judge of his own merit" (*OI,* 106).
4. This idea was already implicit in Rousseau's description of the writing of his reveries: "I shall content myself with keeping a record of my readings without reducing them to a system" (33). Collecting is often something one is engaged in either in childhood or in old age. Some features associated with collecting might lead us to think of it in relation to the register of desire (as though Don Juan were the ultimate collector). For the collector something of the intrinsic identity of the thing, which depended on its belonging to a world, is often lost, and the thing collected is valued solely as another piece in the collection. And yet the condition in which things become devoid of inner meaning and, as it were, cannot speak for themselves anymore might precisely allow for another form of sober and melancholic thoughtfulness, which can be called allegorical. Walter Benjamin links the de-contextualization involved in collecting to such allegorical sensibility:

   > Perhaps the most deeply hidden motive of the person who collects can be described this way: he takes up the struggle against disper-

sion. Right from the start, the great collector is struck by the confusion, by the scatter, in which the things of the world are found. It is the same spectacle that so preoccupied the men of the Baroque; in particular the world image of the allegorist cannot be explained apart from the passionate, distraught concern with this spectacle. . . . in every collector hides an allegorist, and in every allegorist a collector. As far as the collector is concerned, his collection is never complete; for let him discover just a single piece missing, and everything he's collected remains a patchwork, which is what things are for allegory from the beginning. On the other hand, the allegorist—for whom objects represent only keywords in a secret dictionary, which will make known their meaning to the initiated—precisely the allegorist can never have enough of things. With him, one thing is so little capable of taking the place of another that no possible reflection suffices to foresee what meaning his profundity might lay claim to for each one of them. (W. Benjamin, *The Arcades Project*, p. 211)

5. There is a connection between the minimal and the awareness of the surroundings. Minimalist art works make one aware of their bare presence in the place in which they are located. This turn occurs negatively, as an experience of the failure to hold onto something. The minimal is thus strangely equated with the effects of the absolutely great, the sublime.

The affinity drawn between fragment and totality is a characteristic of the Romantic sensibility. See in particular Friedrich Schlegel's "Atheneum Fragments" out of which the following fragment is taken: "A fragment, like a small work of art, has to be entirely isolated from the surrounding world and complete in itself like a hedgehog" (§206). The fragment, on that Romantic conception, is generating a movement of the mind that tends to the expression of the idea. That is, what is lacking in the fragment is not something in particular; instead, its indeterminate lack creates a movement of meaning in the collection of fragments, a movement that can point to the totality.

One can further relate such notions as smallness and totality by way of the idea of a miniature. The miniature is not just the reduction in size of a given thing, but more importantly, it aims to condense significant features in a limited space. In such miniatures meaning becomes fragmentary by being barely hinted, by being abbreviated. This might be the place to note that the *Reveries* is a small book, not just compared to the unending and open-ended *Confessions,* but also in itself. Its walks seem often no more than bagatelles, ending shortly after they have started.

6. In his *Critique of Judgement* Kant elaborates a limit case of the judgment of taste directed upon what he calls "free beauty." It is a judgment giving the imagination total freedom, without a guiding concept. The flower is found among the objects of such a pure judgment. Surprisingly, precisely this judgment comes closer to the domain of the moral than aesthetic judgments in general. This is because the very *existence* of beauty partakes in the enjoyment.

Such a formulation might sound problematic, since for Kant the aesthetic judgment of beauty should not take any interest in the existence of the object it estimates. Yet Kant forms a distinction between the disinterested judgment of taste and the interest in there being disinterested judgments of taste; interest in the very existence of beauty. The flower, as the extreme case of a free judgment of taste, is also a thing of beauty in which one takes an intellectual interest. Such an intellectual interest, which is a sign of a moral constitution, is to be distinguished from the empirical interest in the beautiful, which is the interest in there being communication over the agreement in taste. The beauty of the flower is appreciated in isolation even while manifesting a certain distaste for society: "One who alone (and without any intention of communicating his observations to others) regards the beautiful form of a wild flower, a bird, an insect, or the like, out of admiration and love of them, . . . takes an immediate, and in fact intellectual interest in the beauty of nature. This means that he is not alone pleased with nature's product in respect to its form, but is also pleased at its existence" (*Critique of Judgement,* ak. 299). One might fantasize Kant as having Rousseau's *Reveries* in mind when he adds that such a person "readily quits the room in which he meets with those beauties that minister to vanity or, at least, social joys, and betakes himself to the beautiful in nature, so that he may there find as it were a feast for his soul in a train of thought which he can never completely evolve" (ak. 300). The fate of the flower is to become an example of what Friedrich Schiller, elaborating on that moment in Kant, calls the naïve. Defying the attempts to speak about it, closed upon itself and self-sufficient, the flower is nature that is wholly itself, and thereby also a symbol for a redemptive possibility for man:

> For what could a modest flower, a stream, a mossy stone, the chirping of birds, the humming of bees, etc., possess in themselves so pleasing to us? It is not these objects, it is an idea represented by them which we love in them. We love in them the tacitly creative life, the serene spontaneity of their activity, existence in accordance with their own laws, the inner necessity, the eternal unity with themselves.
>
> *They are what we were;* they are what *we should once again become.* ("On Naïve and Sentimental Poetry," p. 181)

Schiller's understanding of naïve nature is governed by what might be called a symbolic sensibility, in a double sense: first, insofar as he takes the flower to be a symbol of the ideal that man strives toward, a symbol of the second, moral nature, to replace the lost innocence of natural existence; second, insofar as he thinks of the relation of man to the ideal as capable of being presented by such a self-enclosed figure. In that latter sense the notion of symbol marks not so much the disjunction of the sign and the signified as the way in which a transcendent order can be fully incarnated, even if momentarily, in perceptible material. The symbol, in that sense, is an ideal of artistic practice and is to be contrasted with allegory. The first manifests a fullness of expression, a plasticity that allows the paradoxical embodiment of the transcendent; the latter appears to such symbolic sensibility as a mere illustration of concepts.

According to Schopenhauer's understanding of the beauty of the vegetal world, its attraction does not reside in its self-enclosed nature, in its complete disregard for man. Rather, such beauty calls attention or makes advances precisely because of an inherent lack: it lacks the possibility of representation. It attracts because it needs men to represent it, to act as its representatives in the realm of representation. Is this cultivation of meaning, for which the plant's fate is an allegory, something man can hope to bring to fruition? Can man be the one who completes creation by bringing things into themselves, to rest in their nature, in and by means of language? Can the journey from nature to language be completed? Walter Benjamin interprets the Fall as the failure of man to bring nature to fulfillment in language: "It is a metaphysical truth that all nature would begin to lament if it were endowed with language . . .

Lament . . . is the most undifferentiated, impotent expression of language. It contains scarcely more than the sensuous breath; and even where there is only a rustling of plants, there is always a lament. Because she is mute, nature mourns" ("On Language as Such and on the Language of Man" in *Selected Writings*, vol. 1, p. 72). Rousseau's description of his botanical occupation manifests this melancholy relation to nature. If for Schiller a flower is the symbol of morality, then for Rousseau the botanical collection is an allegory of mortality.

7. Certain affinities to Rousseau can emerge in collecting some remarks of Wittgenstein's from the *Philosophical Investigations*. In the preface to that work, Wittgenstein relates the fragmentary nature of his writing and the idea of inclination:

> It was my intention at first to bring all this together in a book whose form I pictured differently at different times. But the essential thing was that the thoughts should proceed from one subject to another in a natural order and without breaks.
>
> After several unsuccessful attempts to weld my results together into such a whole, I realized that I should never succeed. The best that I could write would never be more than philosophical remarks; my thoughts were soon crippled if I tried to force them on in any single direction against their natural inclination." (ix)

It is further striking that the central figure for the work of thinking in that preface is that of walking or journeying: "For [the nature of the investigation] compels us to travel over a wide field of thought criss-cross in every direction.—The philosophical remarks in this book are, as it were, a number of sketches of landscapes which were made in the course of these long and involved journeyings" (ix).

That work of thinking exposes the surface of language, hence shows everything of importance to be on that surface: "Philosophy simply puts everything before us, and neither explains nor deduces anything- Since everything lies open to view there is nothing to explain. For what is hidden, for example, is of no interest to us" (§106). Philosophy fights the sublimation of thinking (§89) by the attention to details: "In order to see more clearly, . . . we must focus on the details of what goes on; must look at them *from close on*" (§51). Details are always multiple and must be assembled or collected as reminders: "The work of the philosopher consists in assembling reminders for a particular purpose"

(§127). A certain rest or repose is to be the end of thinking, what "gives philosophy peace so that it is no longer tormented by questions which bring *itself* in question" (§133).

8. Circles of Destiny

1. Sören Kierkegaard's *Journals and Papers*, vol. 6, ed. Hong and Hong (Bloomington: Indiana University Press, 1970).
2. F. Nietzsche, *Human, All Too Human*, §617 (Cambridge: Cambridge University Press, 1986).
3. "Lettres morales," lettre 6, *Correspondance*, vol. III, p. 369, quoted in Poulet, *Les metamorphoses du Cercle*, p. 112, my translation.
4. In his *In Quest of the Ordinary* Stanley Cavell develops the relation between the notion of fate and being "subject to expression" by way of interpreting Emerson's essay "Fate." Upon reading sentences from that essay, such as "Character teaches above our wills. Men imagine that they communicate their virtue or vice only by overt actions, and do not see that virtue or vice emit a breath at every moment," Cavell writes: "Now it says openly that language is our fate. It means hence that not exactly prediction, but diction is what puts us in bonds, that with each word we utter we emit stipulations, agreements we do not know and do not want to know we have entered, agreements we are always in, that were in effect before our participation in them. Our relation to our language to the fact that we are subject to expression and comprehension, victims of meaning is accordingly a key to our sense of our distance from our lives, of our sense of the alien, of ourselves as alien to ourselves, thus alienated" (p. 40).

The work in and on language necessary to traverse fate, thus the task of reading set by Emerson and Rousseau, is an issue that, I take it, these authors are at odds about. One could call it the difference between the idea of endless responsiveness in the constant transformation of meaning, and an ideal of the actualization of meaning in a final stable state. The conception of such an ideal must address the threat of what Cavell calls a metaphysical interpretation of intelligibility, the danger of confusing "absolute responsibility of the self to make itself intelligible" with "responsibility of the self to make itself absolutely intelligible" (*Conditions Handsome and Unhandsome*, p. xxviii).
5. Tracy Strong adopts a model of authenticity in language that relies on

the primacy of song. "A language that has lost its musicality—its ability to represent emotion while making rational arguments—will be unable to persuade or create real social bonds"(*Jean-Jacques Rousseau: The Politics of the Ordinary*, p. 354).

In support of his claim Strong turns to Rousseau's opera and points out that in the dialogue *Rousseau Judge of Jean-Jacques,* "Rousseau" praises *The Village Soothsayer* for the accord of words and music: "What makes this opera approved by people of taste is the perfect accord of words and music, . . . the musician always thought, felt, spoke like the poet." This appreciation of the operatic voice should be read in relation to the concerns of the *Essay on the Origin of Languages.* It is virtually a definition of opera that it is a passionate, extravagant, and hyperbolic vocalization. Such hyperbole is not manifest in figures of speech but in the very fact of singing. The voice in opera emerges out of passion, as a vocal extension of passion. It is an embodied voice that does not dissociate between the representation and the body that emits it. It is, as it were, a voice that one cannot hide behind.

But the myth of the origin of language speaks also of the return of things to their true size, of being true to the voice while overcoming its excess. To assess whether the singing voice can stand on its own as a paradigm of authentic speech, it might be necessary to consider in more detail the structure of *The Village Soothsayer.*

The opera opens with Colette, the village shepherdess, in despair that her lover Colin is estranged from her and courts city women. Colette turns to the village soothsayer and offers him all her money in exchange for his telling her the fate of her love. The soothsayer instructs her to keep her money and promises to arrange something. As Colin arrives, the soothsayer hides Colette. He then warns Colin that Colette has taken a fancy to the men of the city. Colin becomes anxious, his pride is wounded, and his jealousy flares. He promises the soothsayer to stop his visits to the city if only Colette returns to him. The soothsayer mumbles some magic words and Colette comes out of her hiding place. The lovers are reunited. The opera ends with a country festival in which all the villagers gather to celebrate love's victory in songs and dances.

The opera ends with a chorus in which the virtues of country festivals are contrasted with the degenerate plays, concerts, and operas of the city. This ending in itself is enough to raise what can be called the performative paradox of the opera, for what is the point of the performance of an opera against opera, an opera to end all operas at the King's Court in Fontainebleau? A solution is reflected in the very structure of the opera plot, in the way it achieves resolution: Colin is described as caught in the problematic of self-love that arises out of comparison: by seeing himself in relation to the life of the city Colin becomes blind to his real love. It is also the case that Colin is returned to true love by means of an artifice whose essence is the arousal of those reactive feelings that are tied to self-love, such as jealousy and pride. One could then suggest that this structure of the plot is a reflection of the very function of the performance of the opera. Rousseau writes in his *Emile:* "Much artifice is required to prevent man from becoming entirely artificial." Similarly, the motto of *The Village Soothsayer* could be: "much theater is required to save us from theater."

To reinforce this intuition, consider the place of the central character, the soothsayer, who, importantly, does not have a name. He is the one who pulls all the strings and brings about the reunion of the couple. He is the one who puts on an act in order to let nature shine through. I assume further that we should identify the soothsayer with Rousseau, for he is the only one who sings a song in this opera. (That is, in opera everyone sings, but there are few occasions of *musica in scena* in which a character is actually portrayed on stage as singing). Through this device the soothsayer is identified with the one who produces music, with Rousseau himself. In general, a soothsayer is also characterized by his special relation to language—he doesn't read books, however, but signs in the things themselves. He reads in entrails of animals, that is, a language that does not represent nature but belongs to nature itself. Thus the power of the soothsayer is not only located in the fit of song and content, but also in a certain relation to the visual signs.

The soothsayer makes his singing powers manifest at the end of the opera in a village festival. Thus the opera leads from the problematic of self-love and self-representation to a triumph of love and a social gathering that is very different from the shows of the city. At the same time, this movement leads away from the singing voice to the mutual exposure of the festival. (See in this context the discussion of overcoming representation in Chapter 9.)

6. Rousseau is often portrayed as opposing sensation and reflection and valuing the immediacy of the sensuous. In the *Will to Power* Nietzsche

identifies Rousseau's legacy with "sensualism in matters of spirit." This emphasis on the sensuous is no doubt central to Rousseau's presentation of man in the state of nature. As Starobinski puts it: "Here we have an 'animal' and 'sensationalist' version of the Stoic ideal of autarchy. Man does not look outside himself, nor does he look beyond the present moment. In a word, he lives in the *immediate*. If each sensation is new, the apparent discontinuity is merely a way of experiencing the *continuity* of the immediate . . . Language is scarcely necessary. Sensation has direct access to the world, to such a degree that man scarcely distinguishes himself and his environment" (J. Starobinski, *J. J. Rousseau: Transparency and Obstruction*, p. 25).

Starobinski also identifies in Rousseau an attempt to live a form of sensuous ethics, but thinks it doomed to failure. The bad faith implicit in Rousseau's attempt can be posed as follows: "It is one thing to *submit* to the influence of an environment, another thing to analyze the moral effects of sensory experiences and *shape* the objects around us in such a way that their influence is beneficial. Rousseau wanted to surrender entirely to sensation, but only if the environment was favorably disposed towards him" (p. 212). And further: "A man who sets up a magic show cannot succumb passively to its magic without bad faith. He cannot ignore the fact that he deliberately created what he wants to experience as an independent force" (p. 214).

Now, it is quite clear that the mythical narrative of the state of nature is construed around the opposition of pure sensation and language. But as with the other issues in the myth of the state of nature, the point is always to apply that mythical description to the present conditions of existence, to think of them as mythical descriptions that can be concretized in the condition of having language and society. Thus we must ask how the positivity of the given can turn into the idea of affirmation which characterizes the sphere of meaning. In the *Reveries* that stability is brought to being in memory. It is the given of one's life that must be affirmed, thus not quite something one could set up as one wants. Secondly, the present at stake is not the passing now of sensuous experience, but is to be characterized by way of the notion of full actuality. The idea of actualization and concentration of meaning provides a way to address the excess of meaning without giving up on meaning or giving in to the soothing effects of the sensuous. Thirdly, the idea of concentration also reveals an ethical dimension (not a sensuous ethics) if it is understood that meaning is brought to rest, concentrated, only in reading, that is by others. This is ultimately why Rousseau cannot set up the magic show the way he might have chosen to do.

9. Exposing Theater

1. Already in the "Second Discourse" Rousseau emphasized that self-love arises in internalizing the gaze of others, and mankind takes its first step on the road to inequality as spectacles appear on the stage of human history:

   > People grew accustomed to gather in front of their huts or around a large tree; song and dance, true children of love and leisure, became the amusement or rather the occupation of idle men and women who had flocked together. Each one began to look at others and to want to be looked at himself, and public esteem had a value. The one who sang or danced the best, the handsomest, the strongest, the most adroit or the most eloquent became the most highly regarded. And this was the first step toward inequality and, at the same time, toward vice. From these first preferences were born vanity and contempt on the one hand, and shame and envy on the other. And the fermentation caused by these new leavens eventually produced compounds fatal to happiness and innocence. (*OI*, 64)

2. In my analysis of the *Social Contract* I am indebted to the illuminating and thought-provoking recent work of Steven Affeldt on Rousseau. See his "The Citizen as the Legislator: The Conversation of Constitution in Rousseau's *The Social Contract*" in his "Constituting Mutuality: Essays on Expression and the Bases of Intelligibility in Rousseau, Wittgenstein, and Freud" (PhD. diss., Harvard University, 1996). See also his "The Force of Freedom" in *Political Theory*, vol. 27/3 (June 1999), pp. 299–333.

3. Rousseau's revival in modern political philosophy is primarily a result of John Rawls's reworking of the theory of the social contract in his *A Theory of Justice*. To assess Rawls's adaptation of Rousseau's state of nature and social contract it is fruitful to ask at what level a political concept of expression will find a place in Rawls's theory.

   Expression is not required in the original position—Rawls's recasting of the state of nature. The original position is a device of representation that allows the construction of a deductive argument for the two principles of justice, and since each party has exactly the same information as others, communication between them is neither necessary nor possible. Moreover, Rawls's understanding of publicity in the well-ordered society reduces the need for reciprocal expression, as, presumably, everybody is already in an acknowledged state of agreement over fundamental matters. The theory provides a framework of justification for anyone, allowing to bring one's beliefs at all levels into reflective equilibrium. This is once more a process that each and every citizen can go through for himself or herself.

Although we need not express ourselves about what is shared, expression is essential prior to the constitution of the framework of agreement, in the process of eliciting intuitions implicit in the public political culture. Here we might think of the work of language as that of giving expression to those intuitions, or translating them into a form in which they are acceptable to others on reflection and can do some work, or generate contentful principles of justice. (Rawls's theory is itself an example of such work.)

But expression is not only required to reveal and form the basis of agreement, It is also required to address deep disagreement. Rawls writes:

> That there is no social world without loss is rooted in the nature of values and the world, and much human tragedy reflects that. A just liberal society may have far more space than other social worlds but it can never be without loss. The basic error is to think that because values are objective and hence truly values, they must be compatible. In the realm of values, as opposed to the realm of fact, not all truths can be fitted into one social world. (*Political Liberalism*, p. 197)

Loss, then, seems inherent in any agreement over the basic form of society. The possibility of distinguishing between inevitable loss and violence done to some party to society is contingent on creating a dialogue within society before agreement is reached. It depends on the assurance that all parties have been allowed expression. When loss is a result of being denied a voice, it becomes violence.

The discussion of Rousseau brings out a further concept of expression which is not addressed in Rawls's theory. For there might be a sense of loss that has to do with the very constitution of law, with the potential left out by law itself in its origination—that is, with the loss of nature rather than of a particular form of life. Whereas Rawls presents his theory as an overlapping consensus, what Rousseau brings out is the necessity of expressing the mutually excluded.

Finally, the considerations raised also problematize Rawls's separation of the issue of the form of the institutions of an (ideal) well-formed society, based on the content of the principles of justice, from the issue of stability. Rawls assumes that these issues are separable, making the question of stability a question of the affirmation over time of the institutions that allow the conditions of living in a well-ordered society. Stability is thus essentially an issue of social psychology. But at least according to Rousseau, it might not be possible to separate the question of stability from the contents of the compact to form a society. As he writes towards the end of the "Second Discourse," "the vices that make social institutions necessary are the same ones that make their abuses inevitable" (*OI*, 77). The use of force within society can never be wholly justified, since there is always a relation between the force that is used within a social order, call it preserving force, and the force that was at the origin of the creation of the social order, call it originating force. This relation of the internal and the external is the reason for the decline of every constituted society. For Rousseau, stability is first and foremost related to the act of legislation as a constant reaffirmation of society.

4. In *The Claim of Reason* Stanley Cavell presents Rousseau's writing as exemplary, as "a way to use the self as access to the self's society": "What [Rousseau] claims to know is his relation to society, and to take as a philosophical datum the fact that men (that he) can speak for society and that society can speak for him, that they reveal one another's most private thoughts" (pp. 25–26). Implicit in that relation of self and society is another more troubling possibility: "[Y]ou will have to decide about his bouts of apparent insanity. Are they merely psychological problems? . . . . Or are they expressions of grief that society should conduct itself as it does? Not grief for himself, but for society, which willfully denies knowledge of its own conspiracies, and not just those directed against him" (p. 26). Not only can Rousseau speak for others, but others, speaking for him, can harm him in what is his ownmost sense of self. The dependence on them in being meaningful turns every communication into an intrigue. It is, as Cavell writes, a sign that "we are not expressed in the law we give ourselves, that the public does not

exist, that the social will is partial (conspiratorial)" (*Conditions Handsome and Unhandsome*, p. 31).
   If the starting point of the *Reveries* is the severing of every relationship, how are we to conceive of the exemplification involved in that text? What is the relation that remains between Rousseau and society, between Rousseau and his reader? What is the exemplification of the exclusion? And is the notion of exemplification adequate at all to capture that condition? Is it only negatively, in the gesture of refusal that indicts society, in the insistence on remaining unknown, that Rousseau remains attached to society?
   Rousseau is not representative insofar as his condition is extreme, hardly to be followed. He sets a standard but is not thereby an exemplar. He does not speak "for" society, nor does he allow society to speak for him. The exemplar is "in society," part of a circle of culture, of an ongoing conversation. The standard is solitary, stable and unchanging.
5. As an example of this relation between tragedy and the political, consider Nietzsche's account of the creation of law in *The Birth of Tragedy:*

> Sophocles understood the most sorrowful figure of the Greek stage, the unfortunate Oedipus, as the noble human being who, in spite of his wisdom, is destined to error and misery but who eventually, through his tremendous suffering, spreads a magical power of blessing that remains effective even beyond his decease. The noble human being does not sin, the profound poet wants to tell us: though every law, every natural order, even the moral world may perish through his actions, his actions also produce a higher magical circle of effects which found a new world on the ruins of the old one that has been overthrown. (F. Nietzsche, *The Birth of Tragedy,* p. 68)

6. W. Benjamin, "Language in Tragedy and Trauerspiel," in W. Benjamin, *Collected Writings*, vol. 1.
7. In his *Absorption and Theatricality* Michael Fried has introduced the term "absorption" as the opposite of the theatrical. It serves him to characterize Diderot's antitheatrical sensibility in his writings on the first Paris salons. But the relation of absorption and theatricality is, as Fried's history of art shows amply, a dialectical one.

10. After Words

1. Compare to Nietzsche's riddle opening the first chapter of *Ecce Homo:* "The fortunateness of my existence, its uniqueness perhaps, lies in its fatality: to express it in the form of a riddle, as my father I have already died, as my mother I still live and grow old" (p. 38). See also Thoreau's *Walden:*

   > Books must be read as deliberately and reservedly as they were written, for there is a memorable interval between the spoken and the written language, the language heard and the language read. The one is commonly transitory, a sound, a tongue, a dialect merely, almost brutish, and we learn it unconsciously, like the brutes, of our mothers. The other is the maturity and experience of that; if that is our mother tongue, this is our father tongue, a reserved and select expression, too significant to be heard by the ear, which we must be born again in order to speak. (p. 69)

   Significantly, Rousseau links reading to the consciousness of existence and portrays his father as the one with whom he began to read: "I do not know how I learnt to read. I only remember my first books and their effect upon me; it is from my earliest reading that I date the unbroken consciousness of my own existence. My mother had possessed some novels, and my father and I began to read them after our supper. At first it was only to give me some practice in reading. But soon my interest in this entertaining literature became so strong that we read by turns continuously, and spent whole nights so engaged. For we could never leave off till the end of the book" (C, 19).
2. Michael Davis forms a parallel between Mme de Warens' relation to Rousseau and Rousseau's relation to his reader: "The *Reveries* as a whole is Rousseau's attempt to do for us what Mme de Warens did for him. His soul is meant to become the vehicle for the realization of our souls; this is what it means for Rousseau to be a parent" (*The Autobiography of Philosophy*, 269). To my mind this affirmation of intimacy does not address the essential difficulty of the beginning, Rousseau's complete rejection of all company. To avoid attributing to Rousseau bad faith in opening the book, it is necessary to clarify the nature of the intimacy to which essential distance and irretrievable loss belong, that is, how the beginning and the end of the *Reveries* hold together.

Works Cited

Affeldt, S. *Constituting Mutuality: Essays on Expression and the Bases of Intelligibility in Rousseau, Wittgenstein, and Freud* (Ph.D. diss., Harvard University, 1996).
——— "The Force of Freedom." In *Political Theory*, vol. 27 no 3. (June 1999), pp. 299–333.
Babbitt, I. *Rousseau and Romanticism*. Austin: University of Texas Press, 1977.
Bachelard, G. *The Poetics of Reverie*. New York: Orion Press, 1969.
Benjamin, W. *The Arcades Project*. H. Eiland and K. McLaughlin, trans. Cambridge: Harvard University Press, 1999.
——— *The Origin of German Tragic Drama*. J. Osborne, trans. London: NLB, 1977.
——— *Selected Writings*, vol. 1. M. Bullock and M. W. Jennings, eds. Cambridge: Harvard University Press, 1997.
Blum, C. *Rousseau and the Republic of Virtue*. Ithaca: Cornell University Press, 1986.
Cassirer, E. *The Question of Jean-Jacques Rousseau*, 2nd ed. Introduction, trans., and ed. by P. Gay. New Haven: Yale University Press, 1989.
——— *Rousseau, Kant and Goethe*. Princeton: Princeton University Press, 1970.
S. Cavell, *The Claim of Reason*. Oxford: Oxford University Press, 1982.
——— *Conditions Handsome and Unhandsome*. Chicago: University of Chicago Press, 1990.
——— *A Pitch of Philosophy*. Cambridge: Harvard University Press, 1994.

———— *In Quest of the Ordinary: Lines of Skepticism and Romanticism.* Chicago: University of Chicago Press, 1988.
———— *Senses of Walden.* San Francisco: North Point Press, 1981.
Cranston, M. *The Solitary Self: Jean-Jacques Rousseau in Exile and Adversity.* Chicago: University of Chicago Press, 1997.
Davis, M. *The Autobiography of Philosophy.* Lanham: Rowman and Littlefield, 1999.
de Man, P. *Allegories of Reading: Figural Language in Rousseau, Nietzsche, Rilke and Proust.* New Haven: Yale University Press, 1979.
———— *Blindness and Insight: Essays in the Rhetoric of Contemporary Criticism.* Minneapolis: Minnesota University Press, 1983.
———— *The Rhetoric of Romanticism.* New York: Columbia University Press, 1984.
Derrida, J. *Of Grammatology.* Trans. Gayatri Chakravorty Spivak. Baltimore: The Johns Hopkins University Press, 1976.
Descartes, R. "Meditations on First Philosophy." In *Philosophical Writings of René Descartes,* trans. J. Cottingham et al. New York: Cambridge University Press, 1985.
Fried, M. *Absorption and Theatricality: Painting and Beholder in the Age of Diderot.* Chicago: Universityof Chicago Press, 1980.
Friedlander, E. "Chambery, June 12 1754: Rousseau's Dedication of the Self." In *Political Theory,* 28/2 (April 2000), pp. 254–272.
———— *Signs of Sense.* Cambridge: Harvard University Press, 2001.
Heidegger, M. *The Fundamental Concept of Metaphysics.* Bloomington: Indiana University Press, 1995.
———— *The Principle of Reason.* Bloomington: Indiana University Press, 1996.
Hume, D. "My Own Life." In D. Hume, *Essays, Moral, Political and Literary,* ed. E. F. Miller. Indianapolis: Liberty Classics, 1987.
———— *A Treatise of Human Nature.* Oxford: Oxford University Press, 1978.
Kant, I. "Conjectural Beginning of Human History." In I. Kant, *On History,* ed. L. W. Beck. Indianapolis: The Library of Liberal Arts, 1975.
———— *The Critique of Judgement.* J. C. Meredith, trans. Oxford: Oxford University Press, 1986.
———— "Idea for a Universal History from a Cosmopolitan point of View." In I. Kant, *On History,* ed. L. W. Beck. Indianapolis: The Library of Liberal Arts, 1975.

Kelly, C. "Rousseau's *Confessions.*" In *The Cambridge Companion to Rousseau*, ed. P. Riley. Cambridge: Cambridge University Press, 2001.

Poulet, G. *Les Metamorphoses du Cercle*. Paris: Plon, 1961.

Rawls, J. *Political Liberalism*. New York: Columbia University Press, 1993.

——— *A Theory of Justice*. Cambridge, MA: Harvard University Press, 1971.

Riley, P. Ed. *The Cambridge Companion to Rousseau*. Cambridge: Cambridge University Press, 2001.

Rousseau, J. J. *The Confessions*. J. M. Cohen, trans. New York: Penguin Books, 1953.

——— "Discourse on the Origin of Inequality." In *The Basic Political Writings*, trans. D. Cress. Indianapolis: Hackett, 1987.

——— *Emile*. Introduction, trans., and notes by A. Bloom. New York: Basic Books, 1979.

——— "Essay on the Origin of Languages." In J. J. Rousseau and J. G. Herder, *Two Essays On the Origin of Language*. Chicago: University of Chicago Press, 1966.

——— *Oeuvres Complètes*, vols. I-IV. B. Gagnebin and M. Raymond, eds. Paris: Bibliothèque de la Pléiade, Gallimard, 1969.

——— *Reveries of the Solitary Walker*. P. France, trans. New York: Penguin Books, 1979.

——— "The Social Contract." In *The Basic Political Writings*, trans. D. Cress. Indianapolis: Hackett, 1987.

Schiller, F. "On Naïve and Sentimental Poetry." In *German Aesthetic and Literary Criticism: Winckelmann, Lessing, Hamann, Herder, Schiller, Goethe*, ed. H. B. Nisbet. Cambridge: Cambridge University Press, 1985.

Shklar, J. *Men and Citizens: A Study of Rousseau's Social Theory*. Cambridge: Cambridge University Press, 1985.

Starobinski, J. *J. J. Rousseau, Transparency and Obstruction*. A. Goldhammer, trans. Chicago: The University of Chicago Press, 1988.

Strong, T. *Jean-Jacques Rousseau: The Politics of the Ordinary*. Thousand Oaks: Sage Publication, 1994.

Wittgenstein, L. *Culture and Value*. Chicago: The University of Chicago Press, 1984.

——— *Philosophical Investigations.* G. E. M. Anscombe, trans. Oxford: Blackwell, 1958.
——— *Tractatus Logico Philosophicus.* D. F. Pears and B. F. McGuinness, trans. London: Routledge, 1961.

Index

Accident, 22–23, 27–31, 34–35, 38, 58–59, 73–74, 126
Affeldt, Steven, 148
Autobiography, 1–2, 5, 15–16, 20, 34, 43, 70, 114, 118, 122, 131

Babbitt, Irving, 118
Benjamin, Walter, 7–8, 104, 115–116, 129, 139, 140, 142, 151
Botany, 54–55; chapter 7 passim; 138–139, 143

Cassirer, Ernst, 114–115, 121
Cavell, Stanley, 7–8, 113, 116, 119–120, 128, 144, 150
Chance, 70, 73–74, 111
Childhood, 15, 37–38, 43, 69, 73, 78–79, 95, 99, 128–129, 133, 139
Collection, 5, 72, 75–77, 79, 81–84, 139–140, 143
Concentration, 3, 5–6, 8, 26, 54, 59–60, 81, 86– 87, 89–90, 94, 114, 123, 147–148
Confession, 44, 46–48, 70–72, 130
Confessions, The (Rousseau), 1, 20, 43–47, 70–71, 109
Contract, 10, 18, 20–21, 63–65, 96, 103, 120, 148

Creation, 31, 33, 47, 102–103, 142, 150

Davis, Andrew, 126, 136–137, 152
Decline, 19, 39, 65, 101–103, 150
Dedication, 42–43, 45, 53, 97, 121, 129, 136
De Man, Paul, 130–131
Derrida, Jacques, 7, 124–126, 135
Descartes, René, 7, 11–14, 18, 23, 30–40, 128–129
Detail, 5, 54, 75–76, 80–81, 116, 143
Diderot, Denis, 24, 121, 151
Discourse on the Origin of Inequality (Rousseau), 6, 19, 23, 50, 64–66, 109, 121, 129, 132, 148, 150
Discourse on the Sciences and the Arts (Rousseau), 25
Duty (*see also* Obligation), 96

Emile (Rousseau), 132, 146
Essay on the Origin of Languages (Rousseau), 48, 69, 145
Exemplary (Example), 4, 7–8, 21, 22, 44–45, 71, 97–98, 103, 121, 124, 150–151

157

Index

Existence, 7, 10–12, 16–19, 21–24, 27–35, 38, 50–54, 58–60, 68, 78–79, 86–87, 90, 93, 103, 108, 117, 124, 136, 141, 152
Exposure, 3, 16, 25, 46–48, 69, 71–72, 99–105, 110, 130–132, 143

Fate, 7, 16, 28–29, 70–71, 83; chapter 8 passim; 104, 106, 108–109, 111, 115, 124, 135, 144
Feeling (*see also* Sentiment), 18, 22–24, 31, 36, 50, 58–59, 67, 75, 85–86, 93, 127, 132, 136, 146
Fiction, 15, 45, 47–48, 60, 101, 130, 139
Figure, 4–5, 15, 35, 37, 48–50, 52–53, 55–56, 60, 65, 76, 86–89, 92, 94, 110, 114–117, 142–143, 145
Fragment, 82–83, 107, 140, 143
Freedom, 21, 26–27, 32, 36, 46, 57, 61–63, 67–68, 72–73, 77–78, 88, 102, 127, 141
Fried, Michael, 151

Gaze, 46–48, 50, 69, 88, 90, 104–105, 132, 148
Gesture, 90–91, 110, 151
Gift, 61, 68–69, 72, 135
Given (the), 17, 47, 61, 69, 72–73, 92, 94, 97, 127, 147

Heidegger, Martin, 7, 38, 129, 133–136, 139
Hölderlin, Friedrich, 124, 133–136
Hume, David, 1, 113, 118–119, 137

Identification, 2, 4, 7, 18, 29, 38, 50–51, 65–67, 90, 101, 111, 115, 126
Imagination, 13, 15, 32, 35, 37, 45, 48, 57–58, 60, 77, 80, 82, 88–89, 92, 110, 111, 127, 141

Inclination, 61, 63–65, 67–68, 75, 77–78, 81, 84, 119, 143

Judgment, 15, 17, 47, 70–72, 89, 114, 122–123, 126–128, 133, 139, 141

Kant, Immanuel, 126, 127, 141
Kierkegaard, Soren, 85, 113, 117–118, 144
Kindness, 64, 110–111

Language, 7, 15, 20, 24, 27, 29, 38, 43, 45, 47–51, 65, 69, 76, 82, 88–92, 103, 105, 107, 117, 122–123, 128, 132, 136, 139, 142–147, 149, 152
Letter to D'Alembert (Rousseau), 95–96, 100, 130, 137

Maturity, 37, 39–41, 129, 152
Memory (*see also* Recollection), 13–14, 25–26, 31, 33–34, 36, 40, 43–45, 60, 77, 84, 91–92, 107–110, 147
Miniature, 140

Nature (*see also* State of Nature), 1, 7–8, 11, 19–23, 25, 27, 31, 38, 47, 50, 55, 63–68, 71, 76, 78, 80, 83–84, 95, 102–103, 108, 110, 115–116, 118, 120–122, 127, 129, 131–133, 138, 141–143, 146–152
Nietzsche, Friedrich, 85, 113, 116–117, 124, 144, 146, 151–152

Obligation (*see also* Duty), 43, 45–46, 61, 63, 72–73, 96, 121
Ordinary, 2, 5, 7, 9, 13–14, 16, 21–22, 47, 62, 72, 79, 95, 117–118, 138

Persecution (*see also* Victimization), 22, 42, 44, 89–90, 92
Pity, 63–67, 69, 72, 118

Rawls, John, 7, 148–150
Reading, 2–10, 15–18, 27–29, 43, 66, 72, 74, 94, 104–107, 113–116, 119–120, 126, 132, 137–138, 144, 146, 148, 152
Recollection (*see also* Memory), 6, 13, 17, 27, 60, 75, 81–83
Reflection, 16, 26, 55–56, 58, 61, 65, 79, 88, 125, 146, 149
Representation, 20, 27, 49–51, 67, 95, 97–98, 100–103, 105, 116, 123, 127, 137–138, 142, 145–146, 148, 151
Reverie, 4, 12, 15–16, 18–19, 24, 26–27, 31, 33–36, 39–40, 44–45, 52, 57–60, 75–77, 80, 82, 94, 104, 118–120, 123, 125–126, 128, 136–137, 139
Rousseau Judge of Jean-Jacques (Rousseau), 1, 15, 70, 117, 145

Schiller, Friedrich, 117, 127–128, 141–143
Schopenhauer, Arthur, 142
Self, the, 3, 7–8, 10, 15–19, 22–24, 27–29, 31, 35–37, 40, 46, 50–51, 55, 60, 69, 82, 86–90, 97, 108, 119, 120, 122, 132, 136, 144, 150
Self love, 23, 46, 63–64, 87, 146, 148
Sensation, 22, 59, 79, 93, 137, 146–147
Sentiment (*see also* Feeling), 23, 30, 58, 65, 100, 136
Sentimental, 83, 109–110, 127, 142
Shame, 43, 46–47, 131–132

Shklar, Judith, 120, 122
Social Contract, The (Rousseau), 6, 96, 98, 120, 148
Society, 8, 14, 18–23, 25, 52, 63–68, 72, 77, 98, 99, 101–104, 119–122, 124, 126, 133, 136, 141, 145–151
Solitude, 6, 9–12, 17–21, 39, 52, 68, 77, 93, 95, 104, 108, 114, 117–122, 125–126, 128, 136, 151
Space, 7–8, 10, 14, 17, 24, 27, 31, 34–36, 54–57, 60, 89, 101, 125, 136, 140
Starobinski, Jean, 118, 121, 123, 125–126, 129, 147
State of Nature, 19–20, 23, 50, 63–65, 67–68, 121, 131, 147–148
Strong, Tracy, 120, 137, 138, 144, 145
Surface, 5, 55–56, 58, 72, 77, 79, 95, 110, 143
Surroundings, 35–37, 53, 56, 60, 79–83, 86, 90, 140

Theater, 66–67; chapter 9 passim; 109–110, 121, 137, 146, 151
Time, 13, 24, 29, 34–35, 37, 39–40, 44, 55–60, 88, 91, 97, 104, 125, 129, 133–134, 136, 138, 150
Truth, 1, 2, 4, 8, 13–17, 20, 24, 25–27, 29, 33, 37, 42–49, 51, 60, 63, 69, 70–71, 77, 84, 88–92, 96, 101, 108, 114, 118, 123, 125, 133, 139, 142, 145

Victimization (*see also* Persecution), 21, 28, 30, 44, 70, 72, 89, 122, 144
Village Soothsayer, The (Rousseau), 145–146
Voltaire, 117, 123

Walking, 31, 35, 37–38, 56–57, 61, 118–119, 143
Warens, Mme de, chapter 10 passim; 152
Wittgenstein, Ludwig, 7, 114, 123, 128, 143
World, 3–4, 6, 10, 12–13, 16, 19, 21–24, 27–29, 31–38, 40, 44, 52–60, 62, 80–83, 87, 89–90, 93–94, 101, 108, 113–114, 116–121, 123, 128–129, 131, 133–134, 136–137, 139, 140, 147, 149, 151
Writing, 2, 5, 7, 8, 13–18, 21, 24–29, 41–47, 61, 65–66, 68, 71–73, 75–76, 82, 94, 96–97, 114, 117, 119–126, 128, 130–131, 138, 152